PARTY
ORGANIZATIONS IN
AMERICAN POLITICS

Copublished with the Eagleton Institute of Politics,
Rutgers University

PARTY ORGANIZATIONS IN AMERICAN POLITICS

CORNELIUS P. COTTER
JAMES L. GIBSON
JOHN F. BIBBY
ROBERT J. HUCKSHORN

American Political Parties and Elections

general editor:
Gerald M. Pomper

PRAEGER SPECIAL STUDIES • PRAEGER SCIENTIFIC

New York • Philadelphia • Eastbourne, UK
Toronto • Hong Kong • Tokyo • Sydney

Library of Congress Cataloging in Publication Data
Main entry under title:

Party organizations and American politics.

(American political parties and elections)
Bibliography: p.
1. Political parties—United States. I. Cotter,
Cornelius P. II. series.
JK2261.P314 1984   324.2'1'0973   84-8286
ISBN 0-03-071831-7 (alk. paper)

Published in 1984 by Praeger Publishers
CBS Educational and Professional Publishing
a Division of CBS Inc.
521 Fifth Avenue, New York, NY 10175 USA

456789   052   987654321

Printed in the United States of America
on acid-free paper

Contents

Tables and Figures

Acknowledgments

The research reported in this book was conducted as part of the Party Transformation Study, supported by the National Science Foundation under Grant No. SOC 77-27020. Any opinions, findings, and conclusions expressed are those of the authors and do not necessarily reflect the views of the National Science Foundation.

The Graduate School, the College of Letters and Science, the Golda Meier Library, and the Social Science Research Facility at the University of Wisconsin-Milwaukee contributed to the research in numerous and important ways.

The authors were fortunate in attracting the assistance of extremely talented and energetic staff and students at the University of Wisconsin-Milwaukee and at Florida Atlantic University. At Wisconsin-Milwaukee we wish to thank the political science staff, Gilda Malofsky and Ruth Fefer who helped in myriad ways, and Lois Kohlmetz who cheerfully and competently typed (and retyped) the final manuscript. Mary E. LeBlanc capably performed the duties of project manager, in addition to helping with data collecting and coding.

David Allen, G. Hillis Beck, Robert W. Biersack, Carol M. Burzinski, Patricia C. Hauser, Larry Holt, Paul Michels, Michael Logan, Maureen Rolfs, Ann R. Thomas, and Joan A. Wells performed coding and related chores for which we are very grateful. At Boca Raton, Marilyn Campbell, Richard Kux, and Theresa Sala contributed to the project by performing coding and computer analysis tasks. Christine Mikulski, Carol Monday, Cathy Goetzl and Ann Bendall contributed to the manuscript typing at Boca Raton.

Many of our colleagues across the country kindly provided access to their survey instruments and data. We wish especially to thank Paul A. Beck, William J. Crotty, Herbert Sydney Duncombe, Bernard C. Hennessy, Jerome M. Mileur, and Sarah McCally Morehouse for their generosity in sharing data and materials with us.

The study could not have been completed without the cooperation of thousands of persons active in the organizations of both major parties at levels ranging from national to local. We are especially indebted to the staffs of the Democratic and Republican National Committees who assisted us in identifying state and local party officers and who cordially welcomed us to national committee and executive meetings.

A special expression of gratitude is due to the 53 state party chairs, the scores of state party executive directors, the national committee members, and the governors and liaison staff who so patiently attempted to satisfy the curiosities of probing professors whose interests may at times have seemed arcane in relation to the day's work.

Finally, we acknowledge the courtesy and tolerance that prompted hundreds of former state party chairs, serving from 1960 to 1978, to respond to the questionnaire that we mailed them, and that led thousands of county-level party chairs to respond to a questionnaire mailed to the full universe of local party chairs.

Table 2.5 in Chapter 2 was previously published in a chapter which the authors wrote for Gray, Jacob, and Vines, *Politics in the American States*, and we are grateful to the editors and the publishers, Little, Brown and Company, for permission to reprint. Tables 2.6, 2.7, and 2.8 in Chapter 2 previously appeared in an article written by the authors, in the May 1983 *American Journal of Political Science*; we are indebted to the editor and the University of Texas Press for permission to reprint. Visual Design Services at the University of Wisconsin-Milwaukee produced the figures in the book, and we are grateful for their fine work.

PARTY
ORGANIZATIONS IN
AMERICAN POLITICS

1

Introduction

It became fashionable in the decade of the 1970s to think of American parties as verging upon extinction. Party organizations as such had not been the subject of systematic observation for some decades, but were generally held to be in an advanced state of decay. Party support in the electorate, and, indeed, electoral interest in politics were deemed at their nadir. Political scientists and journalists were prone to cite declining party identification, declining turnout, and a growing disinclination to vote straight party tickets as evidence of erosion of the significance of party, and as clear indication of the probable decay of party organizations.

Realignments and the transition from one pattern of party electoral dominance to a quite different one had come along at generational intervals for about a century, and another was due in the 1960s. Within a few years of appearance of the authoritative work on this process of party transformation (Burnham, 1970), its author announced the end of the realignment process in the United States and the imminence of an era of "partyless politics" (1975, 1976).

The authors of this study were uneasy with much of the commentary and forecasting on political parties and electoral behavior. While they were aware of the evidence on declining allegiance to party in the electorate and lack of discipline among the parties' elected officials, they sensed that predictions of the demise of party and even anticipations of a dramatic realignment of the party system were premature, to say the least. Their backgrounds of service in and scholarly study of party organizations caused them to focus on that part of the scenario of party decline which pertained to parties as organizations. Indeed, in view of a prevalent tendency to ignore or slight party organization in composing essays on party change, it was frequently necessary to ask how this dimension of party could be entered into the analysis.

Earlier research (Huckshorn, 1976; Bibby, 1979, Cotter and Bibby, 1980) and some personal experience suggested that party organizations at the state and national levels did not conform to the conventional perception that they were decrepit, but instead were viable and had grown stronger, not weaker, in the decades since 1950. The evidence from this preliminary research, and a conviction that no informed statements could be made about the status of American parties until data were systematically collected on party organizations across the states, led to the research reported in this book.

The objectives of the research were (1) to gather first hand information on the condition of the state party organizations, both cross-sectionally and over time and, (2) to investigate the relationship of party organizational strength to other aspects of the political process, including electoral success, linkage with officeholders, public policy concerning party, and the extra-party organizations which have proliferated in the electoral arena.

We also wished to explore the significance for party organizations of the role orientations of party leaders. These objectives expanded in the course of the research to take into account the condition of county-level parties, and the patterns of relationship between state party organizations and party at the national and county levels. We were concerned with describing the condition of American party organizations, but the ultimate goal was to contribute to a theory of party change that would take fully into account the role of party organizations.

Although "the great theoretical tradition in the study of political parties was established by men with a distinctly organizational approach" (Sorauf, 1975, p. 36), the role of the party organizations in the process of party and electoral system change has largely been ignored in recent scholarship. Because party organizations are likely to be active agents in such processes, the large questions of realignment, dealignment, and party renewal that preoccupy American political scientists require that attention be given to the role of those organizations.

Where does the party organization fit into such processes? Does a party's organizational strength move in conjunction with changes in its electoral fortunes? Our preliminary research indicated that electoral disaggregation, at least at the level seen in the United States, could proceed concurrently with the strengthening of the party organizations. This suggested that the widely held assumptions about party decline were in need of refinement. It is entirely possible that the revitalization of the party organizations is in part responsible for the failure of the expected realignment to appear on cue about a generation after the critical election of 1932.

Before developing a data base from which to make statements concerning the condition of American party organizations and their role in political processes, it is necessary to develop appropriate concepts and measures to guide data collection. And, as some of the foregoing statements imply, it is necessary to arrive at a clear understanding of the ways in which the concepts interrelate. In short, it is necessary to present a theory capable of generating testable hypotheses.

Party Organizations in the Political Process

Political parties may be conceived in terms of symbols (Epstein, 1980), or as cognitions in the minds of voters (Stokes, 1975), or as teams of candidates (Downs, 1957), but they must also be considered as organizations. As organizations they seek to control the use of the party symbol on the ballot, to exploit the inclination of a segment of the electorate to identify with the party, and to elect candidates nominated by the party. Because they are favored by laws that virtually force the electorate to dichotomized choice, the two major parties in the United States have reasons to expect that by appeals to independents and weak allegiants of the other party they can build electoral victories around their nuclei of faithful supporters.

As election mechanisms, more concerned with nominating and electing than with governing (Schumpeter, 1942; Downs, 1957), American parties emphasize winning office in the short-term. They are also concerned, however, with their own long-term survival. Hence there are limits to the alliances that they will form toward vote-maximizing (Mazmanian, 1970). The long-term concerns of party organizations are reflected in the recent emphasis on sustained financing, the tightening of integrative relationships among party units, and in programs designed to counter the effect of dealigning forces. Nevertheless, if the parties appear to emphasize electing over governing, it does not necessarily follow that they lack interest in the policy outputs of government (Francis, 1968, pp. 21–23). However, the policy process merits the party attention of parties principally as it influences the environment within which they function.

Political scientists have made little systematic effort at addressing the condition of the party organizations as an empirical question. Some twenty years ago, Frank Sorauf observed (1963, p. 2) that " 'party' as an organized recruiter and elector of candidates has been conspicuously missing in many of the recent excellent studies of American voting and electoral politics." This has continued to be the case. The calls for comparative study of state politics that followed V. O. Key's *Southern Politics* (1949) evoked a succession of impressive works on politics in regionally grouped states.[1] This expanding literature has also dealt with the politics of state legislatures (Zeller, 1954; Wahlke, Eulau, Buchanan and Ferguson, 1962; Jewell, 1967, 1982), the politics of gubernatorial leadership (Schlesinger, 1957; Beyle and

Williams, 1972; Morehouse, 1976), voting behavior at the state level (Wright, 1974), and presidential nominating politics (David, Moos and Goldman, 1954). But until Huckshorn's study of state party leadership and organization in 1976, the systematic study of comparative state politics had not extended to state party organizations conceptualized as units for discrete analysis.

The neglect of party organizations may in part be attributed to the flourishing of the voting behavior studies that since the 1940s, produced such an abundance of data on the voting behavior and attitudes toward party politics of the national presidential electorate that political scientists sought in these data the basis for inference about the party organizations. As scholars at the Center for Political Studies (CPS) at the University of Michigan moved into their survey of the 1952 election, one of their objectives was "to study the impact of the activities of the major parties on the population," thus, by implication, seeking the connection between party organizational activity and the behavior of the electorate. However, the authors of *The Voter Decides* conceded this was the "objective least adequately dealt with" (Campbell, Gurin and Miller, 1954, p. 2). The party identification chapter opens with the assurance that the "internal organization, . . . techniques, and activities" of parties have been of enduring interest and much studied over the years; the CPS emphasis would be "to analyze the perceptions, evaluations, and actions of those who identify with them" (pp. 88–89). Although much explicit conceptualization of party and its various components is absent, the CPS party identification scale became a barometer of the condition of the party organizations for the following decades.

If voting behavior studies failed to give due weight to party organization, the positive theorists seeking to generate explanatory theory from a few basic assumptions borrowed from the marketplace or from behavioral psychology simply do not include a place for parties as organizations. Anthony Downs (1957) conceptualizes party as "teams of candidates" and as Joseph Schlesinger points out, "the process by which the team reaches its decisions is assumed away" (Schlesinger, 1965, p. 766). Schlesinger fills this gap with an elegant theory of campaign organizations, based upon the office ambitions of candidates and the incentives of campaign activists (Schlesinger, 1965, 1966). However fruitful Schlesinger's theory is, and replete as it may be with useful implications for the traditional party organizations in the form of local, state and national party committees, it is a theory of campaign organizations, not of party organizations. The designation of the organized effort to win one office one time as a "nuclear party," and the demonstration of the potential for creation of "the multinuclear organization or complex party" through the cooperation of "nuclear parties" (1965, pp. 774, 786), do not bring the traditional party organizations into the theory. The traditional parties, even when they retain an important role in the nominating process, may be peripheral to or even in competition with Schlesinger's "nuclear party" efforts. The aggregation of, or interactions of, such efforts do not define party organization any more than does the aggregation of precinct committee-persons in a state define state party organization.

The fusion of party and candidate that has proven so useful in Downs' *Economic Theory of Democracy* and Schlesinger's *Political Ambition* studies retards the study of party organizations. For example, it obscures the existence of a symbiotic relationship between party organizations and candidates parallel to that which Downs postulates for parties and voters. In American electoral politics the relations of parties, candidates and voters reflect congruity and divergence of interests.

We present here a study of party as an organization having "an internal life of its own" (Sorauf, 1975, p. 37). We do not assume that the strength of the party organization is a mere reflection of other aspects of the party process such as the attitudes and behavior of voters, the performance of partisans in government, the condition of other units of party at the same or at other levels, the changing organizational environment of electoral politics, or the policies designed to govern parties. We do assume that party organizations interact with—influencing and being influenced by—these impinging aspects of the political environment. And, in order to preserve the opportunity to treat these relationships empirically, we must conceptualize party organization to avoid building into our central concept elements that we wish to relate to party organization in a theory of politics.

In this book, we outline a theory of electoral politics in which the party organization plays a central role, and we test a number of hypotheses on the key relationships in the theory. The data collected to permit the hypothesis testing also provide a systematic description of American state and county party organizations. The principal elements in the framework presented here are party organizations, laws pertaining to parties, candidates, officeholders, extra-party organizations, and the electorate, as depicted in Fig. 1.1.

Significant Attributes of Party Organizations

The leading organizational attributes which determine the capacity of parties to operate in the electoral arena are: budget, professional staff, party officers (and their attitudes toward politics), and institutional support and candidate directed programs. Budget and staff determine the capacity of the organization to build and execute programs. Institutional support programs contribute to the durability of the party organization and hence its capacity to influence behaviors and events external to the organization. The relations of

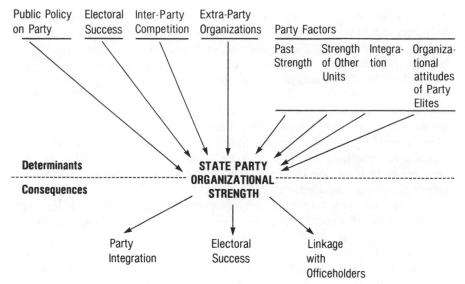

FIGURE 1.1. Determinants and consequences of party organizational strength.

state party organizations to other levels of party, including national and local, are important elements of institutional support programs. Candidate-directed programs pertain to recruiting and support activities in discharge of the party's electoral role.

The changing composition of the participants in the major party organizations and the changing values associated with the party elites will influence the clusters of interests and values associated with the party organizations, and should have some impact on party organizational programs (Wilson, 1962; Kirkpatrick, 1976).

The parties are significant to campaign activists, candidates, and extra-party political organizations because of the assured ballot position of the party, virtually guaranteed by state election law; the advantage parties enjoy in building a popular plurality based on the durable (albeit diminished) core of party voters (e.g. Piereson, 1977); and the material benefits that may be channeled to the party organizations by governments.

Candidates and their Organizations

The aspirant for office requires party nomination and ballot listing under the party label as a condition of aggregating votes for the office. Yet the nominating process may pit aspirant against party organization, or against competitors in a context that gives rise to hostile attitudes toward a neutral party organization. When the nomination is achieved, the party organization and symbol can assure a core of votes, which may also cost them an equal or greater number, hence the candidate's interest may lie in deemphasizing party attachment. The party organization has other resources. It may provide service and funds, but the candidate shares these with other candidates, some of whom may have higher priority, and thus self-interest may dictate creating a separate candidate campaign organization.[2]

The party organization requires candidates. The organization's cardinal goal may be winning office, or it may be survival, but both are contingent upon fielding candidates and winning at least the requisite votes to retain ballot position. If these are absent, it is unlikely that a party organization can attract the resources and maintain the sense of organizational purpose that are requisite to survival. Beyond these minimal levels of significance of candidates to parties, the capacity of the party to function in a competitive electoral system is conditioned to a significant degree on the range and quality of candidates running under the party label. We assume party organizations are committed to electoral competition and election winning.

Thinking at the level of parties interacting electorally with other parties, we find V. O. Key's suggestion that high levels of interparty competition will be associated with strong party organizations persuasive (Key, 1956, p. 132; also see Ranney, 1965, p. 71). Key reasoned that in states in which two-party competition was relatively absent, neither party would have incentive to achieve organizational strength. Conditions in the South have changed somewhat since Key wrote, and it is now entirely possible that the developing (but electorally minority party) in a formerly one-party system will be associated with increasing levels of organizational strength. Hence, high levels of interparty competition, and the status of a party in a system of low interparty competition, may both have a major effect on party organizational strength.

As suggested earlier, we associate successful organizational effort by parties with election winning, and would expect to find that even in today's complex campaign systems with multiple categories of participants in the campaign process, the strength of party organizations will have some impact on the electoral success of the party at specific office levels. Thus, we expect that the relative organizational strength of the parties in a system will find some reflection in the vote.

Officeholders

With victory achieved, at least for the governorship, the party organization may discover that the officeholder perceives a conflict between personal political ambition and party interests. This can lead to keeping party officers and staff at a distance, or even to an effort to weaken the party organization. Alternatively, the governor who undertakes to lead the party, but proceeds to attempt to reduce it to a personal vehicle, may also have a damaging impact. Thus, electoral success magnified to the standing of a victory, does not necessarily confer unequivocal blessings on the organization.

Yet the likelihood is that the party organization will develop and exert a capacity for relating to its officeholders in the legislature and the gubernatorial office, and will meet with success in its efforts to protect itself against adverse legislation and to gain material and symbolic rewards to distribute to party workers. Not the least of the governor's incentives to accept and respond to party linkage efforts is awareness that renomination requires party auspices. Many governors have acknowledged party help in dealing with the legislature and the national administration (Muchmore and Beyle, 1980).

Extra-Party Organizations

Effective party organizations are adaptive—accommodating to change in the poltical environment. It is our assumption that the party organizations, whether or not they may succeed, will attempt to find ways to use electoral innovations, such as the direct primary, to their advantage, or at least to mitigate the harmful effects upon the organization. Hence we reject Key's thesis (1956, Chap. 6), taken up by Pomper (1977), Conway (1981), and others that attrition of functions or activities traditionally performed by parties is necessarily indicative of decay or atrophy of party organization. Key used the metaphor of the volunteer fire department which, shorn of traditional firefighting functions, has become a social group. Apt as the metaphor may be, we do not see the patterns of adaptation of party organizations to changing political environments as leading toward political innocuousness for the parties. And, we see only irony in Sidney Blumenthal's finding ("The Flaw in the Big G.O.P. Machine," *The New York Times*, November 30, 1980, p. 17) that provision of services to candidates renders party organizations mere campaign consulting operations.

Changes in federal law since 1971 have released a flood of organizational influence into the nominating and electoral process, with undoubted consequences for national, state and local parties. Political action committees have joined candidate campaign committees and private management and advisory firms (Malbin, 1980; Sabato, 1981) to make available to prospective nominees and candidates resources that the parties are thought to have once monopolized. The easy response to these developments is to take the general complexity and turbulence of the changing political environment as evidence of the atrophy of parties and decomposition of American politics.

But, the organizational complexity of American life is an old story, going back to Alexis de Tocqueville's observation of "the immense assemblage of associations" in the new nation (Tocqueville, 1946, II: p. 106) and it is not clear that the party organizations will, or that researchers should, be unduly intimidated by recent changes in the listings on the scorecard of electoral politics.[3]

We attempt to trace the relationships between state party organizations and extra-party organizations. But in a period of great change in the number and variety of extra-party organizations functioning in the electoral process, it appears sensible to seek merely to control for Political Action Committee (PAC) activity in testing hypotheses on the relationship between state party organizational strength and electoral success.

Law on Party

We envisage party organizations as having "primacy" in relation to electoral and governing processes. But an equally important aspect of the parties is that they are acted upon by government policies designed to regulate or support them, and by policies that alter the environment of electoral politics in ways that present new challenges to the political parties.

The United States has the most pervasive body of statutory law on political parties and elections of any nation in the world (e.g., Epstein, 1980, p. 44). It is reasonable to expect that these laws have some determinative impact upon the parties. The pace of such lawmaking has stepped up in the past decade at both the national and state levels and the reach has been extended.

We hypothesize that the strength of party organizations is determined in part by regulatory and support features of statute law. That is to say, we expect the effects of such law to offset the impact on parties of dealigning forces. Reciprocally, insofar as the party organizations express interest in policy and seek to influence policy, we expect this interest to focus on legislation pertaining to parties and elections (Francis, 1968).

In addition to enacting laws that have the effect of raising entry barriers to politics and conferring preferred status upon the traditional major parties, the states have been changing the environment of electoral politics in ways that less obviously favor the parties. In addition, the federal government's recent policies have state-level effects that cannot be ignored. The state party organizations of today confront state and federal requirements that candidates set up separate campaign committees, thus formalizing much more the separation between party organizations and candidates. Both state and federal jurisdictions have begun subsidizing election campaigns, with the funding going to the candidates or to the party (Jones, 1980, 1981; Noragon, 1981; Alexander and Frutig, 1982). The federal actions in the 1970s that allowed dramatic increase in the number of political action committees operating in the spheres of nominating and general election politics have shredded any hopes the parties have had "to exclude powerful nonparty elites . . . from a share of the control over the nomination and election process" (Sorauf, 1963, p. 3). Thus, the state of policy on party is in flux, its major thrust not yet clear and the results of our hypothesis-testing may be equivocal.

Summary

If the political machine, which mobilized and disciplined the electorate, candidates, and officeholders, were to represent the acme of American party organization, equivalently strong, if not quite different party organizations would be required to make any kind of impact upon the less tractable politics of today. Contemporary American politics are not characterized by random fractionization; the electorate is not an undifferentiated mass. Less orderly and more complex than in times past, the politics of the state and nation are increasingly two-party rather than one-party if we take into account the leavening impact of contests for federal office and governor upon competitiveness in the states (David, 1972; Sabato, 1983). In balance, it may be more difficult to achieve a stable, dichotomized division of politics today than in times past. All of this suggests to us the possibility that party organizations at the national, state, and local levels, interacting within the party structures and competing within the two-party system, play a significant role in determining the pattern of American politics.

Hence we begin our analysis by assessing the strength of the party organizations, taking into account changes since 1960. In seeking to account for the interactions of the major influencing factors that determine political outcomes, the succeeding chapters will address the relationships between party organizational strength and candidates, officeholders, law on party, and extra-party organizations. We will also examine the relationships among party units and the influence of the attitudes of party elites upon attributes of party organizational strength.

NOTES

1. See Key (1956), Fenton (1957, 1966), Lockard (1959), Heard (1960), Havard (1972); texts include Jacob and Vines (1965 et seqq.), Gray, Jacob and Vines (1983), Dye (1969), Jewell and Olson (1982), and Morehouse (1981).

2. Jewell and Olson (1982) state the relationship between party organization and candidate aptly: "Candidates, parties, and interest groups may be expected to take a pragmatic, even manipulative, view toward each other. Each type of actor may be expected to calculate what it is lacking to achieve a particular purpose, and to consider what resources others possess which would be helpful to the first" (p. 160). "Successful parties outlive their founders and outlast any specific candidate. Further, parties are concerned with, or at least their labels are used for, a wide variety of offices at all levels of government. Thus, parties have a more inclusive and longer-range concern than any one candidate seeking any one office at any one time" (p. 163).

3. Though political organizations have increased exponentially in the last decade, political action committees (PACs) have functioned for nearly half a century, during which they have been mostly the province of labor unions. The pattern of alliance between labor PACs (particularly the Committee on Political Education, AFL-CIO) and the Democratic party organizations during that period suggests the strong likelihood that labor, business, trade association, and ideological PACs will work out shifting patterns of alliance with party organizations, and that the latter will organize and staff to deal with the PACs and attempt to coordinate PAC activities.

2

State Party Organizations: Measurement and Change*

Literature on the urban machine abounds (Sorauf, 1980, p. 71, fn. 9), but relatively little has been written about party organizations at the state and national levels. Permanent party headquarters manned by professional staffs did not appear at the national level until after World War I. Republican National Chairman Will Hays (1918–1921) opened a party headquarters and the Democratic National Committee followed suit in 1928 (Cotter and Hennessy, 1964, Ch. 1). However, the state parties lagged behind the national committees in establishing headquarters operations and it was generally conceded that state party organizations were only marginally "organizations." In 1956, Key (p. 271) noted that it was common to find "almost a complete absence of functioning statewide organization." He further observed that "while no census of the state of state central committees is available, the general impression that most of them are virtually dead is probably not far wrong" (1956, p. 287).

Although the institutionalization of state committees lagged behind the national committees, a notable trend toward professionalized parties was detected in the early 1960s. In 1961, William Prendergast reported that seven Republican state chairmen were fulltime paid operatives and that 36 Republican state committees had permanent headquarters with at least one paid professional staff member. Daniel Ogden (1961) found a similar pattern for the Democratic state committees and by 1957–1958 there were 21 Democratic state committees employing fulltime professional staff per-

*Substantial portions of Ch. 2 appeared in the *American Journal of Political Science* (May 1983) and we thank the publisher, University of Texas Press, for permission to reprint those portions. See Gibson, Cotter, Bibby and Huckshorn, 1983.

sonnel. Fourteen parties had an executive director and four state chairmen held fulltime paid positions.

So far as we can discern, Ronald Weber (1969) and David Olson (1971) were the first to attempt to construct measures that would permit the systematic comparison of party organizations across the states. Olson found (p. 123, 134), that as a "result of extensive interstate variety in political parties . . . few generalizations about all or even most American state parties can be made. Evidence is lacking, research is sketchy, and comparative data are almost nonexistent." Weber and Olson made imaginative use of nonsurvey data to build quantitative and qualitative measures of state party organizational strength, in the effort to offset these limitations. Huckshorn (1976) then contributed to the development of the comparative study of state parties with his interview-based research on the role of the state party chairman. His interviews with state chairs in the early 1970s revealed a further strengthening of state organizations as they developed permanent headquarters, professional staffs, and technical competence to assist candidates and local organizations.

Comparative research on state parties requires that concepts be developed to guide the collection of data and the construction of variables that will permit the comparison of quite disparate parties, and that will permit the testing of hypotheses relating strength of state party organizations to other theoretically relevant attributes of the political process. In this chapter, we present our conceptualization of party organizational strength and report descriptive statistics on state party organizations resulting from the application of the measures derived from that conceptualization.

Concept and Measurement

The central organizing concept for this research is party organizational strength (POS). Strong parties are organizationally complex and have developed programmatic capacity. Organizational complexity requires an enduring headquarters operation with leadership, staff, and budget. The highest level of complexity implies bureaucratization in the Weberian sense (Weber, 1946, p. 196 ff.), that responsibilities, obligations, and tasks associated with positions are clearly defined. Strong organizations must also be capable of sustaining a high level of programmatic activity related to electoral goals. Through such activity the party organization develops a constituency with firm expectations and support, and the organization becomes resilient to disintegrative forces. The programmatic capacity of party organizations helps differentiate them from other political organizations. Thus it becomes important to be able to generate empirically observable indicators of organizational complexity and programmatic capacity as elements of party organizational strength. We report on the construction of these measures in the sections that follow.

In this chapter we report findings on attributes of state party organizations from various sources: interviews with state party chairs and executive directors in 27 sample states; a mail survey to the nonsurvey state chairs not interviewed; and a mail survey of 560 former state chairs who served between 1960 and 1979. The most complete and detailed data on state parties comes from the state chair and executive director interviews. We utilize that data extensively to report on the condition of the state parties from 1979–1980. To analyze change over time, we rely on data from the mail survey of former state chairs. This data is grouped by four time periods: 1960–1964, 1965–1969, 1970–1974, and 1975–1980, allowing us to assess change over the two decade period. Further details on the research design are presented in Appendix A.

ORGANIZATIONAL COMPLEXITY

Accessibility of Party Headquarters

Whether housed in the basement study of an unpaid part-time party chair, or in spacious commercial quarters that are owned or leased by the party, all party organizations exhibit at least the embryo of bureaucratic organization. Almost all state parties today maintain a party headquarters; in the past it was fairly common to find party organizations operating out of the home or business office of the state chair. This was the case for 17 percent of the former state chairs serving in the period 1960–1964. However, this figure dips below five percent as early as 1970 and since then nearly all state parties satisfy at least this minimal requirement for bureaucratization.

The party headquarters must be accessible if it is effectively to serve the various party constituencies. Accessibility is enchanced by:

1. a permanent party headquarters located in a building owned or leased by the party with no shifting of location when a new chair is elected. Of the 54 sample state parties, 91 percent meet this criterion;
2. location in the state capital or in a major city of the state; 80 percent have their headquarters in the capital;
3. maintenance of branch offices throughout the state. Eleven percent met these criteria.

Clearly, within the past few years, headquarters' accessibility has become common and all of the parties are located at the seat of government or in a major population center.

Division of Labor

Complex organizations are adequately staffed and have at least minimal staff specialization in order to effectively utilize their resources. Of the 54 sample parties, 37 percent have fewer than five staff members, making it difficult to envisage much of a division of labor. However, 63 percent have five or more staff members and nearly one-fourth of the parties have 10 or more staffers (mean = 7.2; median = 6.0), thus some degree of specialization is possible for most parties. Size of staff and number of divisions within the party organization are empirically distinct: $r = .52$. The average party has three divisions, although one-fourth have five or more.

State party organizations have become substantially more bureaucratized over the past 20 years. Increasingly, state parties have developed specialized headquarters staffs. In the early 1960s less than half of the state parties had a controller, and still fewer employed public relations directors, research staffs, or field staffs (see Table 2.1). If the functions of these positions were performed, it was by staff members with other assigned responsibilities. However, by the late 1960s a majority of parties had a research staff and only slightly fewer had a field staff. Almost two-thirds had a controller by the early 1970s, and nearly half had a public relations director. These percentages decline somewhat over the course of the decade, but the average number of divisions in the state party headquarters over the time periods from 1960 to 1980 increased by 50 percent.

A similar pattern is observed when overall staff size is considered. The average number of staff in the election years increased by 85 percent from the first to third periods, then declined to a level substantially above 1960–64. Non-election years also show equivalent increases over time. As staffs have become more specialized, they have also become larger.

Party Budgets

Stable, regularized, and adequate financing is required to support a party headquarters operation. Unpredictable funding threatens continuous operation and impedes organizational planning. The average budget for 53 sample state parties is $340,667 (median = $210,000; standard deviation = $420,215). The smallest budget is $14,000 and the largest is $2.5 million. Slightly more than one-quarter of the 53 parties have a budget of less than $100,000. This represents a dramatic increase since the 1960s; non-election year budgets have increased from an average of $188,125 for 16 sample states (1960–1964) to $340,667 for the 53 sample states for which we have 1980 data. Non-sample states have moved from an average of $21,833 in the early 1960s to $185,529 in the most recent period. While the Consumer

TABLE 21.
State Central Committee Staff Size and Specialization.

| | All Staff (average number) | | Divisional Units (average number) | Staff Specialization (percent of parties) | | | | | |
	Nonelection Years	Election Years		Executive Director	Controller	Publicity Director	Research	Field Staff	N
1975–1980	5.9	7.7	2.5	49.7	57.1	32.0	38.8	36.7	147
1970–1974	6.8	8.5	2.7	66.7	62.7	44.0	53.3	40.0	75
1965–1969	4.9	7.6	2.4	52.5	45.8	39.0	52.5	45.8	59
1960–1964	3.5	4.6	1.6	51.2	41.5	29.3	26.8	14.6	41

Data base: Former State Chair and current (1979–80) non-sample State Chair survey responses, and Sample Party Chair interview responses.

17

Price Index (CPI) rose during that period by 275 percent, we do not think that the increased budgets of the most recent period should be discounted as heavily; indeed we think that the budget increases reflect significant moves toward organizational complexity even after some discounting for inflation.[1]

Parties with larger budgets are not, however, more likely to have regularized sources of funding. Treating direct mail, dues, state government subsidies, and special programs such as "Dollars for Democrats" as regular sources of funds, 41 percent of the average state party budget is drawn from regularized sources (standard deviation = 27%). Over 21 percent of the parties derive 10 percent or less from these sources, while only about four percent derive 90 percent or more.

Professionalization of Leadership Positions

The last subdimension of complexity is the degree of professionalism of headquarters' leadership positions. The most highly bureaucratized party organizations have a full-time salaried state chair and an executive director; exhibit at least a minimal level of tenure stability among the professional staff; and are headed by a chairperson who operates with some autonomy from the party's central committee.

A large majority of state party organizations are staffed by a full-time salaried executive, an obvious requisite to effective headquarters organization. Over 90 percent have either a full-time state chair or an executive director. This is a substantial change from the early 1960s when 63 percent of the reporting state parties had either a salaried state chair or an executive director. The proportion of state chairs who serve on a full-time basis increased modestly, but the employment of executive directors increased dramatically from 1960 to 1980. Moreover, the salaries of paid state chairs have nearly doubled since 1960. Based on these measures, nearly all state parties may be classified as highly bureaucratized.

Limited turnover of professional staff is likely to contribute to the flexibility and adaptiveness of an organization, but high levels of turnover will be incompatible with effective operation. A degree of tenure stability is, therefore, an important component of professionalization. The most stable party had only two state chairs between 1960 and 1980; the least stable had 12. The average for all parties is seven. The tenure stability measure also reflects the average tenure of the current headquarters professional staff. For 46 percent of the parties, the average is two years or less. There are three probable reasons for this relatively short tenure of professional staff in state party headquarters:

1. staffing itself is relatively new, and some state parties have only recently found themselves in a financial position stable enough to employ staff on a regular basis;
2. salaries and fringe benefits are comparatively low, thus contributing to high turnover;
3. employment opportunities with non-party groups are expanding.

The third component of professionalism is the extent of autonomy of the state chair from the state committee. Organizations that are professionally managed are characterized by extensive delegations of authority and responsibility from the oversight and policy deliberative body (the state party committee) to the chief executive. The state chairs were asked to indicate areas in which they need state committee support before acting and also to characterize their overall independence from the committee. These items were used to create a trichotomy with the following distribution: quite dependent (13 percent); relatively dependent (19 percent); and relatively independent (69 percent).

These measures of organizational complexity suggest that the state party organizations are much more highly organized than has commonly been thought. Nearly all operate a headquarters, most have substantial organizational resources, and a large portion of the remainder exhibit some degree of bureaucratization.

PROGRAMMATIC CAPACITY

If organizations, even those that are highly bureaucratized, are to survive they must develop reliable bases of support. Party organizations generate support by making themselves useful to constituencies. Structure is mainly important since it contributes to the development of regularized, programmatic activity which generates support for the organization and provides the party with a *raison d'etre*.

We distinguish two types of programmatic activity, institutional support activity and candidate-directed activity. Some institutional support activity is directly concerned with sustaining the organization (e.g., fundraising and services to local party organizations). Other such activity promotes the organization by enhancing its usefulness to candidates and other political actors (e.g., generalized electoral mobilization programs). Institutional support programs enhance the capacity of the party organization to perform as a service bureau for a broad clientele and thus to generate broad support. On the other hand, candidate-directed activity is focused much more specifically and frequently is exclusionary. Services are directed to a particular set of the party's constituency (candidates for office) and such activity is frequently targeted to a subset of candidates.

Institutional Support Activity

Five types of party activity fall into this category:

1. fundraising;
2. electoral mobilization programs;
3. public opinion polling (excluding polling for particular candidates);
4. issue leadership;
5. publication of a newsletter.

Fundraising activity here is conceptualized not as the amount of money generated, but in terms of the diversity of sources on which the party relies for funds. Diversification stabilizes income, but it is also indicative of systematic effort to generate money. Party executive directors were asked to identify the proportion of the party budget derived from nine different sources. Sample state parties averaged 2.7 sources of funds and only 14 percent placed heavy reliance on only a single source. Three sources (major events, direct mail, and large contributions) are relied on heavily by the state parties. Insignificant proportions of their budgets are derived from contributions from non-party organizations, the national party, and member dues. Most of these parties have well diversified sources of funds.

Electoral mobilization programs are quite common among the state parties. Over two-thirds of the sample parties operate an ongoing voter identification program, registration drive, or get-out-the-vote program (independent of such efforts on behalf of specific candidates). In the early 1960s, programs of this sort were somewhat less common, with only 39 percent of the former state chairs from that period reporting mobilization programs. However, by the early 1970s, the proportion of parties with such programs had increased to 70 percent and change since then has been minimal.

Opinion polling is somewhat less widespread with 32 percent of the sample parties regularly conducting polls in election and non-election years, and another 23 percent polling only in election years. A substantial increase in polling occurred from the early to late 1960s, with little change since 1970.

A measure of the party role in the development of issues was constructed from two sources. The first was responses of chairs to the question of whether issue development is left up to candidates. The second as the sample party executive directors' reports on the amount of attention paid to platforms by the headquarters staff. The responses do not confirm the expectation that the role of the parties in this area is slight since in 43 percent of the parties the executive directors reported that "a great deal of attention" is given to the party platform, and 50 percent are involved in the development of campaign issues. When we shift to the former state chair data, the issue leadership role of the parties does not appear to have changed significantly during the 20 year period. The proportion of parties reporting they engage in issue development independently of candidates varied within the range of 27 to 32 percent during that period, with slightly higher activity reported in the second decade. The significantly higher level of activity reported by the sample state parties may indicate recent change, or more likely is an artifact of sampling and interviewing.

The last component of institutional support activity is the publication of a newsletter. The publication and distribution of a party newspaper or newsletter are not trivial enterprises and they do serve important functions. Such journals are the chief source of internal party news for workers and members. They can be used to generate support for the chairperson or the governor, and their party or government policy initiatives. They also often include direct appeals for money, announce fundraising events, and provide printed forms for internal party dues-checkoff systems. There is no doubt that party publications continue to occupy an important position in the area of internal party communications. It is relatively rare to find a contemporary state party that does not publish a newsletter of some sort. Only one-fifth of the parties do not issue newsletters, and even in the early 1960s they were published by two-thirds of the parties.

Candidate-Directed Activity

The second type of programmatic activity focuses more specifically on candidates and includes five major components:

1. financial contributions to candidates;
2. provision of services to candidates;
3. invovlement in the recruitment of candidates;
4. involvement in the selection of convention delegates;
5. preprimary endorsements.

Activity of this sort is beneficial to party organizations not only because it contributes to winning office, but also because it cultivates an important clientele for the party organization. Independent campaign organizations may gain in strength without threatening party organizations if the parties still provide vital candidate support.

The average state party in the contemporary period contributed money to candidates for two of the following five offices: governor, statewide constitutional office, U.S. House, U.S. Senate, and state legislature. Of 53 state parties reporting, 40 made contributions to some candidates, with the aggregate level of contribution for all offices averaging $135,500. The emphasis on party contributions can be measured in terms of the campaigns to which parties most frequently contribute, and the campaigns receiving the highest levels of party support. Contributions were most often given to candidates for congressional office (48 percent), followed by gubernatorial candidates (47 percent), candidates for state legislature (47 percent), candidates for statewide constitutional office (44 percent), and U.S. senatorial candidates (25 percent).

However, when the median amount given to candidates is considered, the rank order of offices is as follows: governor, state legislature, U.S. House and Senate (tied), and statewide constitutional offices. Thirteen percent of the parties contributed to candidates for all five offices.

The pattern of state party contribution to candidates has changed over the 20 years since 1960. This change is revealed in Table 2.2, which reports the percentage of parties making no contribution to various categories of campaigns. For governor and U.S. senator, there has been a sharp drop in the proportion of parties providing financial support in campaigns. While party support for these offices has diminished, there has been a significant increase in the proportion of parties aiding state legislative campaigns and a modest increase in the frequency of party support of congressional campaigns. The percentage of parties making no contribution to any candidates peaked in 1965–69, fell dramatically in the first half of the 1970s, and rose again late in the decade. These longitudinal data tell us nothing about levels or effects of party contribution. However, they do reflect a change in office emphasis to substate races.

The second component of candidate-directed activity is the provision of services to candidates. Nine types of services were provided:

1. advertising and media assistance;
2. accounting/compliance assistance;
3. public opinion polling;
4. research (including research on opponents);
5. registration/voter identification/turnout;
6. staff assistance;
7. literature/phones and direct mail;
8. fundraising;
9. seminars on campaign techniques.

TABLE 2.2.
Percent of State Parties Reporting no Contributions to Candidates.

	Governor	Other State Constitutional Offices	U.S. House of Representatives	U.S. Senate	State Legislature
1975–1980	41.7 (144)	35.9 (143)	39.6 (144)	57.7 (163)	40.6 (165)
1970–1974	21.9 (73)	27.4 (73)	33.8 (74)	50.0 (74)	25.7 (74)
1965–1969	35.1 (57)	36.8 (57)	40.4 (57)	35.1 (57)	40.4 (57)
1960–1964	25.0 (40)	26.7 (30)	42.5 (40)	37.5 (40)	52.5 (46)

Data sources: See Table 2.1
Ns in parentheses

Great variability exists in the breadth of services provided to candidates. In the 1975–80 time period, 89 percent of the state parties conducted campaign seminars for candidates and/or their managers. This represented a considerable improvement over the 1960s when only half of them offered this form of campaign assistance. The increased number of such seminars probably resulted from copying national committee efforts of this kind that began in the early 1960s and was also a result of more sophisticated, although less understood, campaign techniques involving polling, computerized research, and the electronic media. The smallest level of candidate support was in fundraising where only 19 percent of the state parties provided assistance in the late 1970s. It has become common for the state organizations to provide all of the other seven services to candidates with approximately half engaged in each of the activities.

Leaders of the sample state parties assured us that parties are also active in assisting with the recruitment of candidates. The majority of parties recruit candidates for two or more of six state and local offices. It is most common for parties to recruit for state legislative races (65 percent) and quite rare to recruit candidates for gubernatorial races (11 percent). To some degree, the activity level is inversely related to the desirability of the office, with many state chairs noting that one aspect of the job is dissuading potential candidates from running.

A substantial decline in the breadth of recruitment activity may have taken place in the late 1970s. Of the categories of public offices surveyed, the state parties recruited candidates for an average of 3.5 offices in the early 1960s. This figure is relatively constant until the close of the 1970s, at which time it dropped to 2.6 offices. The percentage of parties not involved in recruiting gubernatorial candidates doubled from 1960 to 1980. The differences are not as severe for some of the other offices, but in no instance are more parties active today than in the past (Table 2.3). This may reflect a decline in the need to recruit candidates, or it may reflect changing priorities in targeted offices. For instance, while our data reveal a sharp decline in the proportion of parties recruiting candidates for gubernatorial races over the 20 year period, only a slight decrease in the proportion of parties recruiting for state legislative races was registered.

The decline in gubernatorial recruitment may be related to the increasing competitiveness of races for that office across the states (Sabato, 1983, p. 116 ff.) with increased competitiveness generating more candidates for the nomination. The shift in focus from governor to legislators may mark an increase in the amount of recruitment effort by the state parties, since there are nearly 7,500 state legislative seats in the U.S. Since we do not have measures of total recruitment effort, such an inference from the changing breadth of recruitment must be drawn with caution.

TABLE 2.3.
Candidate Recruitment: Percentage of State Parties Recruiting Candidates for Federal and State Office.

	Governor	Other State Constitutional Office	U.S. House of Representatives	U.S. Senate	State Legislature	N
1975–1980	55.2	58.2	64.4	43.8	79.5	146
1970–1974	64.9	59.5	70.3	63.6	86.5	74
1965–1969	75.4	77.2	82.5	66.7	86.0	57
1960–1964	76.3	73.7	76.3	64.4	92.1	38

Data sources: See Table 2.1

Preprimary endorsing is another approach to influencing the results of the nominating process (McNitt, 1980; Morehouse, 1980). Nearly half of the parties in the sample states reported that they engage in such endorsing, with 28 percent reporting they make formal endorsements and an additional 22 percent noting they endorse informally.[2]

Parties can also relate to candidates by influencing the delegate selection process (since national convention delegates have become proxies for candidates), although party organizational influence on the selection of delegates to the national convention is severely constrained by national delegate selection procedures. Few of the state chairs reported having any influence over the processes for selecting delegates, and nearly one-half reported no influence of any sort. Democratic state chairs were somewhat more likely than Republicans to report that they had no influence (52 vs. 42 percent), but they were also more likely to report that they had high influence (15 vs. 8 percent).

These indicators of programmatic activity reveal that party organizations have experienced two decades of growth. Compared to the early 1960s, state parties in the late 1970s were more likely to maintain electoral mobilization programs, to conduct public opinion polls, to provide services to candidates, and to publish newsletters. Little change has taken place in party involvement in issue development. Preprimary endorsements are slightly more common today than in the past. In financial support to candidates, candidate recruitment, and influence over the selection of delegates to the national conventions, the pattern of party activity has changed significantly and levels of activity have diminished. Yet even these measures do not sustain a conclusion contrary to that which we draw from the overall programmatic activity data, that state party organizations in the late 1970s were substantially more active than in the past.

Party Differences in Organizational Strength

Substantial differences between the parties exist on these indicators of organizational strength. The best discriminator between the two parties is the breadth of recruitment activity. The average Democratic organization recruits for only one office (most typically the state legislature), whereas Republicans recruit candidates for three different offices (most typically state legislature, U.S. Congress, and statewide constitutional offices). The greatest disparity between parties in recruitment is found in the Northeast, but all regions reveal substantial Republican-Democratic differences. For example, though 70 percent of the Republican organizations recruit candidates for Congress, only 22 percent of the Democratic organizations do so.

Many other differences can be documented. As expected, Republicans have larger budgets and staffs, offer substantially more services to their candidates, and are more likely to engage in public opinion polling (74 vs. 35 percent), however they are less involved in issue leadership (especially in the South). Indeed, on only one of the indicators of party organizational strength are Democratic organizations even minutely stronger than Republicans. Seventy percent of the Democratic organizations have voter mobilization programs, whereas 67 percent of the Republican organizations have such programs. The atypical Democratic advantage here reflects that party's traditional emphasis on maximizing turnout. Generally, interparty differences are so substantial that when 14 organizational strength variables are used as predictors of party, 85 percent of the organizations are correctly classified as either Republican or Democratic (canonical correlation = .76).

Having specified the indicators of the concept of party organizational strength, reported descriptive data on these attributes of state parties for the decades of the 1960s and 1970s, and compared the two parties along these strength dimensions, it is now necessary to empirically validate these variables as measures of party organizational strength. The 12 indicators of party organizational strength were, therefore, subjected to factor analysis.

This analysis, which is presented in Appendix B, demonstrated that the 12 indicators are unidimensional. Three initial factors emerged, and a higher order factor analysis performed on these factor scores resulted in a single factor accounting for 75 percent of the observed variance. This factor serves as our summary measure of party organizational strength.

By combining each party's component scores on the elements of organizational strength (Gibson, et al., 1983), it is possible to assign composite party organizational strength scores. We have done so for the 90 parties for which they are available, as shown in Table 2.4.

Frank Sorauf (1980, p. 77) calls attention to the prevalence of the perception that the Republicans tend to have the edge on the Democrats in organization building:

> Both journalists and scholarly observers have noted that the Republicans find it easier to build centralized, cohesive parties than do the Democrats. Why? Two chief explanations suggest themselves. The first has it that the Democrats are more often the majority party, and as such bring together a more mixed and varied coalition than do the Republicans. The explanation seems plausible, but Jewell and Olson control to some extent for party competitiveness and still find the difference between the two parties. (It is true, though, that even in a Republican state the Democrats are still the majority party in the sense of national party loyalties.) The second explanation—one both more elusive and more intriguing—posits a

TABLE 2.4.
State Parties Ranked by Organizational Strength, 1975–1980.

Weak		Moderately Weak		Moderately Strong		Strong	
.000	Vermont-D	.252	Ohio-D	.504	Georgia-D	.774	Oklahoma-R
.079	Mississippi-D	.259	Indiana-D	.509	Minnesota-D	.777	Washington-R
.085	Louisiana-D	.278	Nevada-D	.513	Tennessee-R	.785	Nebraska-R
.148	Illinois-D	.287	Arkansas-D	.522	Rhode Island-D	.798	Wisconsin-R
.185	Tennessee-D	.301	Iowa-D	.525	Virginia-D	.808	Ohio-R
.233	Alaska-D	.324	Delaware-D	.535	California-D	.809	South Dakota-R
.247	Massachusetts-R	.326	New York-D	.553	Missouri-R	.825	Pennsylvania-R
		.342	Idaho-R	.562	South Dakota-D	.825	North Dakota-D
		.352	West Virginia-D	.572	Wisconsin-D	.906	Minnesota-R
		.368	Massachusetts-D	.573	Illinois-R	1.000	Pennsylvania-D
		.386	North Carolina-D	.578	New Hampshire-R		
		.392	Utah-R	.582	Connecticut-R		
		.398	Wyoming-D	.586	Arizona-R		
		.400	Kansas-D	.595	North Carolina-R		
		.405	Colorado-D	.604	New Mexico-R		
		.406	Kentucky-R	.605	South Carolina-R		
		.416	Montana-D	.608	Iowa-R		
		.419	Wyoming-R	.610	Nevada-R		

.419	Missouri-D	.612	Florida-D
.421	Connecticut-D	.626	Nebraska-D
.421	Rhode Island-R	.632	Virginia-R
.421	New Hampshire-D	.632	Mississippi-R
.430	South Carolina-D	.635	Montana-R
.433	Vermont-R	.645	Maine-R
.448	Idaho-D	.651	Texas-R
.450	Maryland-D	.654	Kentucky-D
.456	Arizona-D	.659	Michigan-R
.457	Louisiana-R	.661	Kansas-R
.458	Texas-D	.663	Indiana-R
.464	Maine-D	.681	Colorado-R
.465	Washington-D	.693	California-R
.477	Oregon-D	.695	North Dakota-R
.480	Hawaii-R	.712	Florida-R
.481	West Virginia-R	.716	Oregon-R
.489	Utah-D	.721	Alabama-R
		.737	Georgia-R
		.742	New York-R
		.742	Michigan-D

Note: 90 parties in 49 states are scored. Missing are: Alabama-D, Alaska-R, Arkansas-R, Delaware-R, Hawaii-D, Maryland-R; New Jersey-D, R; New Mexico-D, Oklahoma-D.

TABLE 2.5.
Organizational Strength of Democratic and Republican State Parties,
1975–1980.

Party organizational strength score	Number of state parties[a]		
	Republican	Democratic	Total
.750–1.000 (Strong)	8	2	10
.500–.749 (Moderately strong)	27	11	38
.250–.499 (Moderately weak)	9	26	35
.000–.249 (Weak)	1	6	7
Totals	45	45	90

[a]Data were available for 90 of the 100 state party organizations.

From John F. Bibby et al., "Parties in State Politics," copyright © 1983 by John F. Bibby, Cornelius P. Cotter, James L. Gibson, and Robert J. Huckshorn, in Virginia Gray, Herbert Jacob, and Kenneth N. Vines, eds., *Politics in the American States: A Comparative Analysis, 4th ed.* Reprinted by permission of Little, Brown and Company.

difference in values and traditions between the two parties. The Republicans, the argument goes, are more willing than the Democrats to accept central authority and leadership in the party, more willing to accede to the need for a unified party stand and less likely to dissent and generally kick up a fuss within the party.

Our data confirm this impression, generally that Democratic state party organizations are substantially weaker than their Republican counterparts. Table 2.5 shows that 73 percent of the parties in the strong or moderately strong category are Republican, while 76 percent of the weak to moderately weak parties are Democratic. Furthermore, the disparity in Republican and Democratic strength does not vary by region, reflecting uniform Republican dominance. Within both parties, regional differences in organizational strength are also pronounced.

Table 2.6 summarizes change in the various dimensions of party organizational strength over the period 1960 to 1980. Care must be exercised in interpreting the data in this table because the number of parties represented in each of the time periods differs. While there is certainly variability in the patterns of change in several indicators, it is quite difficult to find much supporting data for the thesis that party organizations have weakened. Indeed, on most indicators, the contrary conclusion is warranted.

Change in Party Organizational Strength, 1960–1980

Over the decade of the 1960s, both Democratic and Republican state party organizations became somewhat stronger. Since then there has been a slight increase in Republican strength and a slight decline in Democratic strength. Table 2.7 displays this trend, employing a scale with an empirical range of roughly −3.00 to +3.00. However, the data in Table 2.7 obscure substantial differences in the patterns of change within the regional parties. Table 2.8 reports organizational strength means for each time period for the eight regional parties. In the early 1960s, great regional and party differences existed. The strongest regional parties were the Democratic parties of the Midwest, followed by midwestern Republicans. Although it may seem surprising, virtually no differences existed between the parties in the South during this period. The traditionally dominant Democratic party had never found it necessary to organize and Republican organizational efforts were only just beginning. Democratic party organizations in the West were substantially weaker than western Republican parties. Interregional differences in both parties were very pronounced for this period, although they were slightly more substantial for Republicans than for Democrats.

No single pattern of change characterizes the regions and parties. As expected, southern Republican parties have changed the most dramatically, from a condition of very little organizational strength to one of above average strength (despite some decline during the 1970s). Midwestern Democratic organizations exhibit a substantial decline in party strength from the early to late 1970s. The most stable parties are the western Republicans, a group exhibiting only modest change in party organizational strength since the early 1960s. Their Democratic counterparts declined somewhat in the 1960s, but then became stronger throughout the 1970s. In none of these regions is there evidence of the continuous decline in the level of party strength commonly thought to have occurred (with the arguable exception of the northeastern Democrats). Generally, Republican state parties in all four regions show greater organizational strength today than in the early 1960s, while Democratic parties in the four regions exhibit a more mixed pattern. Furthermore, the Republicans also exhibit less variation within regions.

Although interparty differences within each time period are fairly substantial, the trend through the early 1970s was one of diminishing differences between the parties. The party organizational strength variables discriminate well between Republican and Democratic organizations, permitting the correct classification by party in 76 percent of the cases in the early 1960s, 73 percent in the late 1960s, and 63 percent in the early 1970s. By the late 1970s, however, the figure increases to 78 percent, suggesting a slight widening of interparty differences. The patterns are not identical within each region, but around 1970 most Democratic state party organizations

TABLE 2.6.
Change in Indicators of Party Organizational Strength.

Indicator	1960–1964	
	Democrats	Republicans
Number of staff divisions—	1.4	1.8
Mean (range: 0–5)	(17)	(24)
Services to Candidates—	47.1	37.5
Providing no service (%)	(17)	(24)
Leadership professionalism—	47.1	29.2
Without a paid full-time headquarters leader (%)	(17)	(24)
Voter mobilization programs—	35.3	41.7
With a Program (%)	(17)	(24)
Public opinion polling—	11.8	33.3
Engaging in polling (%)	(17)	(24)
Size of budget (categories)—	.7	2.3
Mean (range: 0–10)	(15)	(17)
Size of staff—	2.3	4.5
Mean (range: 0–20)	(15)	(17)
Publication of a newsletter—	70.6	62.5
Publishing (%)	(17)	(24)
Money contributions to candidates—	2.7	3.6
Mean (range: 0–6)	(17)	(23)
Headquarters accessibility index—	5.4	5.6
Mean (range: 0–10)	(17)	(24)
Candidate recruitment index—	3.9	3.2
Mean (range: 0–6)	(17)	(23)
Issue leadership—	29.4	25.0
Uninvolved in Issue Development (%)	(17)	(24)

Note: The numbers in parentheses are the numbers of cases (state parties) on which the scores for the indicators are based.

Source: Table 1, at p. 209 in Gibson, Cotter, Bibby and Huckshorn, "Assessing Party Organizational Strength," *American Journal of Political Science*, (May 1983), pp. 193–222.

(continued next page)

began a period of decline. Republican organizations in some regions, like the Midwest, exhibit similar change but generally Republican parties have not declined as precipitously. Thus, the Republican organizational advantage today reflects both Republican growth and recent Democratic decline.[3]

Within each party, regional differences in organizational strength have diminished significantly over time. The percentages of variance in the organizational strength of Republican parties that are explained by regional variables has declined from 68 to 10 over the four periods, and for the

1965–1969		1970–1974		1975–1980	
Democrats	Republicans	Democrats	Republicans	Democrats	Republicans
2.2	2.6	2.4	2.9	1.7	3.1
(25)	(34)	(27)	(48)	(66)	(81)
20.0	11.8	25.9	6.3	16.7	3.7
(25)	(34)	(27)	(48)	(66)	(81)
28.0	20.5	22.2	8.4	15.1	6.1
(25)	(34)	(27)	(48)	(66)	(81)
64.0	55.9	66.7	72.9	68.2	80.2
(25)	(34)	(27)	(48)	(66)	(81)
48.0	58.8	55.6	62.5	30.3	70.4
(25)	(34)	(27)	(48)	(66)	(81)
1.3	2.3	1.4	2.3	.9	2.6
(21)	(30)	(24)	(44)	(60)	(77)
4.3	5.3	5.2	6.2	4.5	7.0
(21)	(30)	(24)	(44)	(60)	(77)
68.0	73.5	63.0	70.8	69.7	81.5
(25)	(34)	(27)	(48)	(66)	(81)
3.0	3.5	3.5	4.1	2.6	3.5
(24)	(33)	(27)	(47)	(66)	(81)
6.2	6.0	6.7	6.9	6.5	7.0
(25)	(34)	(27)	(48)	(66)	(81)
3.4	3.8	3.0	3.5	2.0	3.1
(24)	(33)	(27)	(47)	(66)	(81)
20.0	20.6	29.6	18.8	33.3	40.7
(25)	(34)	(27)	(48)	(66)	(81)

Democrats the decline is from 56 to 10. This pattern of declining regional difference began in the mid-1960s for the Republicans and was characterized by a leveling upward as weak Republican organizations became stronger. The decline in regional differences among Democratic parties did not develop until the late 1970s and was characterized by a leveling downward.

This analysis reveals that party organizations scored substantially higher on the organizational strength measures at the close of the 1970s than in the early 1960s. In terms of the generally accepted thesis of party decline, these data have startling implications: the year in which *The American Voter* appeared (1960) marked the beginning of a decade or more of growth for party organizations. As subjective party attachments weakened in the 1960s and 1970s, the level of party organizational strength increased.

TABLE 2.7.
Change in Levels of Party Organizational Strength.

Organizational Strength Factor Score	1960–1964	1965–1969	1970–1974	1975–1980
Democrats				
Mean*	− .87	− .00	− .06	−.48
Standard deviation	1.15	1.17	1.01	.89
N	15	21	24	60
Republicans				
Mean*	− .47	.19	.33	.41
Standard deviation	.92	1.02	.93	.74
N	17	30	14	77

*Range: −2.6–+2.0. Overall mean: 0; standard deviation: 0.996. High scores indicate greater organizational strength.

Source: Table 3, p. 211 in Gibson, Cotter, Bibby and Huckshorn, "Assessing Party Organizational Strength," *American Journal of Political Science*, (May 1983), pp. 193–222.

Implications for Party Change

Party organizational strength has important implications for a theory of party change and the thesis of party decline. Of course, we do not claim that the condition of the party organizations is equivalent to the condition of the party system. We readily concede that a number of important forces and trends relevant to party change (the declining partisanship of the electorate, the growth of amateurism among party activists, the popularization of candidate selection, and the separation of candidate campaign organizations from party) have materialized over the past two decades. It is even possible that the functional competitors to party organizations have increased in strength more than the party organizations themselves, in effect bringing about a decline in the relative influence of party organizations over the political process.

But the implications of these forces and trends must be understood within the context of party organizations that are currently strong and not weakening. Strong party organizations have been effective in counteracting adverse public policy and the departisanization of the electorate, thus making the party system more resistant to anti-party dealigning influences. The threat to party from extra-party organizations may have increased in the past decade but strong organizations are capable of functional adaptation to ameliorate the anti-party impact of competitive organizations. The recent efforts of the national party organizations to coordinate Political Action Committees (PACs) may illustrate such adaptation. To say more on these

TABLE 2.8.
Regional and Party Change in Organizational Strength.

	Party Organizational Strength Factor Score*											
	1960–1964			1965–1969			1970–1974			1975–1980		
Region and Party	$\bar{X}$	SD	N	$\bar{X}$	SD	N	$\bar{X}$	SD	N	$\bar{X}$	SD	N
Northeast												
Republicans	−.84	.31	3	.15	1.00	7	−.18	1.16	14	.13	.88	15
Democrats	—	—	0	.15	1.53	3	−.47	.54	6	−.56	1.00	15
Midwest												
Republicans	.19	.77	6	1.23	.43	6	.74	.65	15	.72	.70	26
Democrats	.57	.87	3	.87	.64	9	.90	1.12	8	−.11	.90	16
South												
Republicans	−1.63	.41	4	.02	1.20	7	.81	.36	6	.41	.62	16
Democrats	−1.77	1.22	5	.06	.00	1	−.94	.41	4	−.89	.99	13
West												
Republicans	−.03	.47	4	−.28	.81	10	.09	.81	9	.23	.66	20
Democrats	−.85	.31	7	−1.05	.71	8	−.36	.32	6	−.44	.50	16

*Range: −2.6–+2.0. Overall mean: 0; standard deviation: .966. High scores indicate greater organizational strength.

Source: Table 4, p. 212 in Gibson, Cotter, Bibby and Huckshorn, "Assessing Party Organizational Strength," in *American Journal of Political Science*, (May 1983), pp. 193–222.

empirical relationships requires additional data and analysis. But any future development of a multivariate theory of party system change must give appropriate emphasis to the condition and role of the party organizations.

NOTES

1. Our belief that the state party budgets have not been adversely affected by inflation to the extent that the Consumer Price Index (CPI) might indicate has two bases. The first has to do with the nature of the CPI measure, and the second is the trends shown by other related data which we treat as indicators of party organizational strength.

The CPI was designed with the urban wage earner and consumer in mind. During the bulk of the period covered by the Party Transformation Study, the major elements in the CPI were housing, with an emphasis upon purchase of housing (weighted at 33.23 percent of the total index); food (22.43 percent), health and recreation (19.45 percent), transportation (13.88 percent), and apparel and upkeep (10.63 percent). (U.S. Department of Labor, Bureau of Labor Statistics, Handbook, Bulletin 1910, 1976, p. 91, Table 2.). In the twenty year period 1960–1980, medical costs led the increases in the CPI items which pushed the index upward. Cost of medical care increased 336 percent during this period, followed by housing at 292 percent, food at 289 percent, and transportation at 279 percent, with apparel just about doubling in price levels. (Derived from Economic Report of the President, 1983, Table B-52, p. 221.) Housing has the most direct relevance of any of these items for the party organizations, followed by transportation. Food, medical care and apparel are of consequence only insofar as they influence the salaries paid to staff, and we believe the staff salaries of state party organizations failed to keep abreast of inflation during this period, and fringe benefits were just about nil. While the CPI is a standard inflation indicator, used to calculate adjustments in allowed expenditures and in subsidy entitlements under the Federal Election Campaign Acts (see 2 U.S.C. 441a(c)), we do not think it has inherent value for measuring the increasing costs of party organizations, although it has obvious pragmatic utility for adjusting campaign expenses and subsidies.

As we examine associated data presented in the chapter, the evidence of party growth of resources in the face of inflation is overwhelming. For example, non-sample state budgets have increased eight-fold from an average of $21,833 to $185,529 from the first to last periods of the study. The numbers of paid professional staff have increased during the period of the study, and the overall numbers of staff also increased during this time. There is no doubt the parties suffered from inflation during this period, but there is considerable evidence that if the inflation retarded the rate of growth, it did not atrophy growth. One hint of party organizational strategies to reallocate budget priorities in order to protect the capacity for organizational growth in a period of inflation may be found in the data showing increases in party institutional support activities concurrently with declining party support for candidates.

2. Using Jewell's (1983, Tables 1 and 2) enumeration of state parties which endorse as our guide, 10 of the 54 sample state parties endorsed under state statutes during the period of our interviews, and five of the state parties endorsed under party rule (we omit the California Republican Assembly and Democratic Council from the category of party endorsing since we treat these as extra-party organizations). This means that 18.5 percent of the sample parties are in states with endorsing statutes and an additional 9 percent endorsed under party rule, for a total of 27 percent endorsing. The apparent inflation of the endorsing reports from our respondents probably reflects the form of the question. The state chairs were asked "Does your state party have either a formal or informal procedure for pre-primary endorsements?" It would appear that many parties have formal or informal internal procedures for endorsing, in the absence of state statutes or party rules on the matter.

3. Regional and party differences may make the data reported in Tables 2.7 and 2.8 suspect. Because data for all 100 state parties are not available for each time period, the group of state parties for which we do have data must be considered a non-random sample. The overall period means may therefore be affected by the particular mix of state parties within each of the time periods. (Technically, without random sampling we are not entitled to assume that error is randomly distributed with a mean of zero.) For instance, Republican state parties are typically stronger than Democratic parties so a higher frequency of Republican organizations within any particular time period will inflate the period mean. Similarly, since regional differences are pronounced, the mix of regions within each period can substantially affect the average score. Moreover, there is variability in the party-region character of each of the period samples. For instance, the percentage of parties with valid data which are in the South are 27, 18, 13, and 21 for the four periods, respectively. Given the importance to the question of change in party organizations for understanding party tranformation, it is necessary to introduce some control for the particular mix of state parties at each period.

Our strategy for accomplishing this control first requires the estimation of the party and regional effects on party organizational strength. Because the effects may differ over time and because party and region interact with each other, the strength measure was regressed on regional dummy variables, separately for each party within each of the four periods. The results of these regressions are shown on page 38.

While there are several interesting aspects of these results, our interest here is in using these 32 coefficients to project mean organizational strength scores for the 100 state parties in each of the four periods. The results of this projection strongly confirm the trend noted in the uncorrected data. The unadjusted mean organizational strength scores for the periods from 1960 to 1980 are: $-.66$; $+.10$; $+.19$; and $+.10$. For the entire 100 state parties the means are: $-.55$, (87 state parties), $+.17$, .10, and $-.05$, respectively.

Because this question is so important, an additional analysis of the "paired" periods has been conducted, using only state parties for which we have data at two adjacent points in time where change between each of the four periods can be assessed. Change can be gauged by the change in the mean strength score of the parties.

REGRESSION OF STRENGTH ON REGIONAL DUMMY VARIABLES

	Midwest	South	Northeast	West		
			Regression Coefficients			
	b_0	b_1	b_2	b_3	R^2	N
1960–1964						
Republicans	.19	−1.82	−1.03	− .22	.68	17
Democrats	.57	−2.35	−1.43	*	.56	15
1965–1969						
Republicans	1.23	−1.21	−1.07	−1.51	.29	30
Democrats	.87	− .81	− .72	−1.92	.58	21
1970–1974						
Republicans	.74	.07	− .92	− .65	.22	44
Democrats	.90	−1.84	−1.37	−1.26	.52	24
1975–1980						
Republicans	.72	− .31	− .59	− .49	.10	77
Democrats	−.11	− .78	− .45	− .33	.10	60

*Too few cases for analysis.

CHANGE IN AVERAGE STATE PARTY STRENGTH SCORES BY PERIOD

	1960–1964	*1965–1969*	*1970–1974*	*1975–1980*
1960–1964	1.00	+.97* (10)	+.45 (5)	+.91* (12)
1965–1969	+.35 (6)	1.00	−.00 (9)	+.04 (20)
1970–1974	+.68* (7)	+.26 (11)	1.00	+.01 (28)
1975–1980	+.48* (12)	−.03 (14)	−.34 (22)	1.00

Note: Scores for Democratic state parties are shown in the lower left triangle; Republican scores are shown in the upper right triangle. The entries are the differences of the means in the two periods defining the cell.

*$p < .05$, one-tailed test.

These data reveal that:

1. None of the entries for the Republican parties dips significantly below zero. Only one of the Democratic entries is substantially less than zero (change from the early to late 1970s) and it is not statistically significant.
2. For both Democrats and Republicans, two of the six entries are positive and statistically significant (despite the small Ns).
3. The conclusions about the specific nature of change within this twenty year period vary depending upon which of the entries is considered. But examination of the changes in adjacent time periods suggests that Republican organizations peaked around the mid-1960s and then have remained stable. Democratic organizations peaked somewhat later, but experienced some decline in the late 1970s.
4. While the Ns are small, if we compare the parties' scores in the early 1960s to their scores in the late 1970s, we conclude that for both Democrats and Republicans there has been a statistically significant increase in strength.
5. No matter what challenges can be made to these interpretations, there is no evidence to suggest that the party organizations have declined in strength.

3

Local Party Organizational Strength

We tend to think of politics as centered in the state and national capitals. Yet that is not where the population is, nor are more than a small fraction of the 490,000 elective offices in the United States to be found at those levels. Vital as presidential and statehouse politics may be (and hypertrophic as presidential politics may be in shaping our understanding of political processes), it is in the localities that the voters are found and electoral politics conducted. What happens in the 3,600 county and equivalent jurisdictions determines the politics of states and the nation. Indeed, many of these county-level jurisdictions are more populous and more economically significant than entire states, and the politics of such counties may also dominate the states that enclave them. Therefore, it is important to assess the condition of party organizations at this level, to see how these parties articulate with the state and national parties, and to understand their role in the political process.

Although case studies of parties at the substate level proliferate, there is only one earlier project from which findings on party organizations at the county level can be properly generalized to the nation as a whole (Beck, 1974). There are many good reasons for this paucity of data, but the fact is that the generation of systematic data on the nature of party organizations must be considered to be "pre-behavioral" in its level of development (Wahlke, 1979).

In this chapter we draw upon data from a survey of the 7,300 county level party organizations in the United States.[1] Details of the research design for this study are to be found in Appendix C and the basic attributes of the county chairs and their organizations are shown in Tables 3.1 and 3.2.

Our objectives in conducting the study are as follows:

41

TABLE 3.1.
Attributes of County-Level Party Leaders.

Attribute	Democrats[a]	Republicans[b]
Percentage female	19.1	24.2
Percentage non-white	2.2	0.3
Average age, in years	49	49
Percentage high school diploma or less	20.4	16.1
Percentage with education beyond bachelor's degree	34.1	31.1
Median years lived in the county	32.4	27.0
Percentage receiving a salary as chair	2.0	0.9
Percentage assuming chair since 1975	62.0	59.0
Percentage member of state committee	32.8	35.8
Median hours worked		
–election period	12.1	12.1
–non-election period	2.3	2.5
Percentage who will seek another term as chair	49.7	42.6
Percentage aspiring to higher office		
–party office	33.9	34.9
–public office	41.0	38.9
Percentage holding party office before becoming chair	57.1	56.2
Ideological self identification (percentage)		
very liberal	4.2	0.1
liberal	14.8	0.7
somewhat liberal	23.1	2.5
moderate	29.2	15.8
somewhat conservative	20.4	34.5
conservative	7.2	37.2
very conservative	0.9	9.1
other	0.2	0.1

[a]Maximum Democratic $N = 1984$.
[b]Maximum Republican $N = 1872$.

- the extension of the party organizational strength concept to local party organizations
- the presentation of data on the current levels and correlates of organizational strength of county-level parties
- the consideration of longitudinal data relevant to the question of how these organizations have changed over time.

TABLE 3.2.
Attributes of County-level Party Organizations.

Attribute	Democrats[a]	Republicans[b]
Median number of chairs since 1969	2.5	2.6
Percentage with complete set of officers	90.4	80.9
Percentage with year-round office	12.0	13.7
Percentage with telephone listing	11.2	16.3
Percentage with paid full-time staff	3.0	4.0
Percentage with paid part-time staff	5.0	5.6
Percentage with regular annual budget	19.9	31.3
Percentage operating a campaign headquarters	55.4	59.9
Median number of county committee meetings—1978	6.5	6.2
Median number of county committee meetings—1977	5.8	5.2
Percentage with a constitution, charter, or set of rules	68.2	68.3

[a]Maximum Democratic $N = 2021$.
[b]Maximum Republican $N = 1980$.

Organizational Structure and Activity

The conventional wisdom among political scientists and party watchers has held that county and precinct organizations have great difficulty in filling their leadership positions. However, that is not supported by our data. Few of the local party organizations are unable to fill their major leadership positions since over 80 percent of the Republican parties and 90 percent of the Democratic parties (1979–1980) have a complete set of officers. Precinct-level organizations are similarly successful in filling their leadership positions. County-level party chairs were asked to report the percentage of precincts in which the precinct leader position was filled. The median of the percentages reported for the Democrats was 95 percent and for the Republicans 85 percent. Since county committees so frequently are composed of precinct committeemen and women, the correspondence between the levels of filling the precinct and county posts is hardly surprising.

Regular communication occurs among these local party leaders, with most of the organizations scheduling county committee meetings bi-monthly or more often. Of course, the major positions of leadership are almost exclusively held by part-time volunteers and it is extremely rare for a county

TABLE 3.3.
Tenure of Local Party Chairs.

Number of Chairs (1969–1980)	Number of County-level parties	Percent
One	604	18.7
Two or three	1,865	57.7
Four or five	635	19.6
Six or more	128	4.0
Total	3,232	100.0

chairperson to receive a salary. The part-time nature of the position is illustrated by the fact that the median hours worked per week in election periods is 12 and in non-election periods is two.

Furthermore, there appears to be little structural support for the organizations since under 10 percent of the party chairs report any full or part-time paid staff. Only slightly more of the organizations operate a headquarters on a year round basis, and indeed only 11 percent of the Democratic and 16 percent of the Republican organizations have a telephone listing. Approximately one-fourth have a formal budget, although Republicans are more likely to have a budget than Democrats (31 percent versus 20 percent).

The only evidence of widespread formal structure encountered is that approximately two-thirds of the parties have a constitution, charter, or set of rules. It is likely that the number of local parties with formal rules or charters increased substantially with the adoption of the Democratic Party Charter in 1974. The Charter required that all state parties adopt rules and specified norms to guide all state parties in processes pertaining to presidential selection. Many state parties influenced local parties similarly to adopt formal written rules.

These data suggest that in contrast to the state organizations, which normally employ a full-time executive director, the local parties are highly personalized, with little or no bureaucratic structure. But this lack of structure should not be taken to imply that the organizations are unstable or ephemeral. The evidence points to limited turnover in the leadership positions of these parties. When asked to report the number of persons holding the position of chair between 1969 and the time of the survey, the Republicans responded with a median of 2.6 and the Democrats with a median of 2.5 (Table 3.3). These turnover rates are considerably below those for state party chairs, thus the unbureaucratized county parties exhibit considerable leadership continuity. These organizations are also quite durable with only 13 percent of the Democratic chairs and 27 percent of the

TABLE 3.4.
Campaign Season Activities of Local Party Organizations

Activity	Percentage of Parties Reporting Such Activity	
	Democrats[a]	Republicans[a]
Distributed campaign literature	78.8	78.5
Arranged fundraising events	70.6	68.2
Organized campaign events (e.g., rallies)	67.6	64.7
Contributed money to candidates	62.3	69.8
Organized telephone campaigns	60.6	64.4
Publicized party & candidates by buying newspaper advertising	62.2	61.8
Distributed posters or lawn signs	58.7	61.9
Coordinated county-level campaigns	56.8	55.9
Publicized party & candidates by preparing press releases	54.6	54.5
Sent mailings to voters	46.6	58.5
Conducted registration drives	56.0	45.1
Organized door-to-door canvassing	49.4	47.5
Publicized party & candidates by buying ratio/TV time	33.6	32.5
Utilized public opinion surveys	10.6	16.4
Purchased billboard space	9.6	12.6

[a]Maximum Democratic $N = 2021$
[b]Maximum Republican $N = 1980$

Republicans remembering a time in the recent past when the party was not organized in the county. Continuity is also enhanced by the strong tendency for the chairs to be long term residents, with the median number of years lived in the county for Democrats at 32 and Republicans at 27. The absence of formal organization is to some degree mitigated by the longer tenure of the party leaders.

Nor does the lack of bureaucratic structure necessarily imply a low level of programmatic activity. During the campaign season, a majority of both the Democratic and Republican organizations maintain a party headquarters. Table 3.4 shows the frequency of a variety of campaign related activities for both Democratic and Republican organizations. First, it should be noted that virtually no party related differences exist. It is also apparent that most of these activities are conducted by a majority of the parties. The median number of activities among the Democrats is 7.8; for the Republicans it is 7.9. While not all activity should be treated as equally important, it is obvious that many of these require significant organization and resources. It is also apparent that the party organization's role is frequently one of coordinating and organizing, rather than executing. Certainly these data suggest that the county-level parties are far from lethargic.

We would expect the local parties to be involved in campaigns for office and to maintain relations with candidates and their campaign organizations. Asked about the frequency of such participation, the local party chairs indicated it is common at the county, state, and congressional levels (somewhat more so for Democrats than for Republicans), but less frequent at the city and local levels (Table 3.5). The high incidence of non-partisanship in election to local office undoubtedly accounts for some of the discrepancy between party participation in planning and strategy meetings for campaigns for city and local office, and those for county and higher offices (Hawley, 1973).[2] These data suggest that candidates and their campaign organizations are not isolated from the party and reinforce the image of the local parties as coordinating agencies.

Local party involvement in candidate recruitment is also common, principally for state legislature and county offices. Although there is some differentiation between the parties, on the whole there are few party based differences (Table 3.6). Only 17 percent of the Democratic and Republican organizations fail to engage in any efforts to recruit candidates for these offices. If, as Jewell and Olson (1982, p. 100) assert, recruitment activity is "an important litmus test of the existence and activity of party organizations," then most county-level parties pass the test. Moreover, 28 percent of the Republican and 32 percent of the Democratic organizations offer organizational support to endorsed candidates in the primaries. These data depict county-level parties that are, or attempt to be, a significant force in electoral politics. Lists of party voters are maintained by almost all of the precinct organizations in both parties and a slight majority of them are generally effective in getting out the vote. Subjective perceptions may not be perfectly equivalent to objective reality, but there are some indications of viable precinct organizations in these local chair reports.

Both parties are also actively involved in patronage decisions, the Democrats a bit more than the Republicans. Local Democratic organizations are typically involved in local patronage (63 percent), followed by state (58 percent) and national (39 percent). This involvement is commonly in the form of recommending candidates for jobs rather than the more traditional local clearance of candidates. The only difference between the parties is that the Republicans are slightly less involved in patronage decisions than are their Democratic counterparts.

In Chapter 2 we suggested that bureaucratization is probably a condition of programmatic development for state parties. However, for the county-level parties, our empirical findings indicate that substantial amounts of activity, particularly during campaign periods, are associated with

TABLE 3.5.
Local Party Coordination with Campaign Organizations.

	Level of Participation in Candidate Planning and Strategy Meetings (percent)					
	"Often"		"Sometimes"		"Never"	
Office	Democrats	Republicans	Democrats	Republicans	Democrats	Republicans
City & local	25	22	28	28	47	50
County	43	41	34	31	23	29
State legislative	44	39	39	37	17	24
Congressional	31	27	45	42	24	31
Gubernatorial	30	24	42	39	27	37

Maximum Democratic $N = 2021$
Maximum Republican $N = 1980$

TABLE 3.6.
Local Party Involvement in Candidate Recruitment.

	Levels of Involvement in Candidate Recruitment (percent)										
	"Very Involved"		"Somewhat Involved"		"Not Involved"	
	Democrats	Republicans	Democrats	Republicans	Democrats	Republicans
County	38	42	31	29	31	29
City/Town	18	19	26	26	56	55
State Legislature	40	44	33	31	26	24
Congressional	25	27	37	37	38	35

Maximum Democratic $N = 2021$
Maximum Republican $N = 1980$

consistently low levels of bureaucratization.[3] We think the apparent discrepancy is to be accounted for by the varying levels of activity sustained by party organizations at the two levels. Unlike local parties, state parties sustain programmatic activity in off years and election years and sponsor programs designed to stimulate organization and activity by other levels of party. This requires higher levels of bureaucratization than are normally characteristic of the local parties which fit Duverger's description of the "caucus":

> . . . [T]he activity of the caucus is seasonal: it reaches its peak at election times and is considerably reduced in the intervals between ballots. In short the caucus is semi-permanent by nature: we no longer have an ephemeral institution, created for a single electoral campaign and destined to end with it: neither do we yet have a completely permanent institution, like the modern parties for whom agitation and propaganda never cease (Duverger, 1954, p. 18).

Having specified the indicators of the concept of local party organizational strength, and reported descriptive data on the attributes of strength, it is necessary to validate empirically these variables as measures of party organizational strength. To this end, twelve indicators of party structure and program were subjected to Common Factor Analysis (see Appendix D for details). Three factors emerged from this analysis but they were so strongly interrelated as to suggest the utility of treating party organizational strength as a unidimensional concept. Therefore, a second order factor analysis was performed revealing a single factor accounting for 83 percent of the variance in the three-factor correlation matrix. Factor scores from this second order factor analysis serves as a summary indicator of the organizational strength of the local party organizations.

Correlates of Local Party Organizational Strength

In our analysis of the strength of state party organizations in Chapter 2, it was determined that Republican organizations are significantly stronger than their Democratic counterparts. No such finding emerges for local party organizations with the average score for local Democratic parties at +.003 and for Republican parties at −.003. The standard deviation for the Republican organizations is slightly larger than that for Democratic organizations (1.03 versus .88), suggesting slightly greater Republican diversity. Generally, party differences are insignificant.

We have seen that substantial regional differences exist in the strength of the state party central committee organizations. Significant regional differences are observed for the local organizations as well, although the

TABLE 3.7.
Regional Differences in Organizational Strength of State and County Parties.

	Northeast	Midwest	South	West	Standard Deviation
State (1975–1980)					
Republican	+.13	+.72	+.41	+.23	.74
Democratic	−.56	−.11	−.89	−.44	.89
County (1979–1980)					
Republican	+.31	+.15	−.48	+.23	1.03
Democratic	+.35	−.02	−.33	+.08	.88

Range for state parties −2.6 to +2.0.
Range for county parties −2.0 to +2.9.

regional patterns are dissimilar (Table 3.7). Within the Democratic party, the strongest local party organizations are found in the Northeast followed by the West, Midwest, and South. The regional rank order for Democratic state party organizations is the Midwest (substantially stronger), West, Northeast, and South. Republican local organizations are also strongest in the Northeast, followed by the West, Midwest, and South. At the state level, the ranking of Republican organizations is the Midwest (substantially stronger), South, West, and Northeast. Thus, the divergence of state and local regional pattern is greater for Republicans than for Democrats. The South is particularly noteworthy. The Republican state party organizations of the South are the second strongest of the eight state party regions, while the Republican local party organizations of the South are the weakest of the eight local party regions! However, unlike the findings at the state level, region is a significantly better predictor of party organizational strength than is party.

It is likely that local party organizational strength reflects local traditions and ways of doing things more than does state party organizational strength. State parties, as less labor intensive organizations, can more readily develop as bureaucratic and programmatic units. National party committee programs for party building may also contribute to the strength differential between state and local units. Given the concerted effort by the Republican National Committee (RNC) (Cotter and Bibby, 1980; Bibby, 1981) since the mid 1970s, and the absence of an equivalent effort from the Democratic National Committee (DNC), it is possible that the contrast explains a part of the organizational strength advantage that Republican state parties have over Democratic parties. It is also likely that the electorally weaker of the two parties will emphasize organization as a way of addressing the problem of attracting votes. As we have reported in Chapter 2, Republican state party organizations in the South became dramatically stronger over the period of the 1960s to 1980. This development was quite possibly a result of the various "southern strategies" of the Republican National Committee and national Republican leaders. But Republican efforts at building strong local parties have achieved substantially less success, just as their efforts at penetrating southern legislatures have largely failed. Local traditions of party attachments and of local party practice serve as a major impediment to change, resulting in strong regional patterns.

Consequently it is not surprising that the hypothesis that state party organizational strength is associated with local party organizational strength is not supported. When local party organizational strength scores for each party are aggregated to the state level (Table 3.8) and correlated with the state party organizational strength scores, the correlations are weak. For Republicans, the resulting correlation is +.18; for Democrats it is +.19; indicating only a very slight tendency in the hypothesized direction. While there are many causal models compatible with these weak correlations, it generally seems that the factors causing state and local party organizational strength are dissimilar.

It should be noted that there is a strong correlation between the average local organizational strength scores of the two parties $(r = +.77)$, again supporting the interpretation that local factors cause local party organizational strength. This strong correlation, of course, also means that state-level factors are correlated with average local party organizational strength at the same level for both Democratic and Republican organizations. For instance, states with large proportions of their work force unionized are likely to have strong Democratic local party organizations $(r = +.47)$, and strong Republican local party organizations $(r = +.47)$.[4] Generally, it is the larger, industrialized, and somewhat wealthier states which have the strongest local party organizations.

Finally, we note that the local organizations of both parties are dramatically stronger in the "major county" subsample.[5] The mean organizational strength score for major counties is nearly one and one-half standard deviations above the mean strength score for all counties. Again, there is little party difference in the organizational strength of local parties in major counties.

Change in Levels of Party Organizational Strength

Former state party chairs were asked to recall information on their state party organizations during their periods of leadership. From their responses we were able to amass data permitting comparison of the state party organizations over time. This approach is clearly not feasible for the 7,300

TABLE 3.8.
States Ranked by Average Strength of Local Party Organizations

	DEMOCRATS			REPUBLICANS	
Rank	*State*	*Strength*	*Rank*	*State*	*Strength*
1	New Jersey	1.441	1	New Jersey	1.581
2	Pennsylvania	1.033	2	New York	1.107
3	New York	.962	3	Indiana	1.004
4	Delaware	.899	4	Pennsylvania	.943
5	Indiana	.794	5	Maryland	.872
6	Rhode Island	.783	6	Arizona	.810
7	Ohio	.752	7	Ohio	.782
8	New Hampshire	.650	8	California	.705
9	Connecticut	.626	9	New Mexico	.688
10	Illinois	.599	10	Connecticut	.649
11	Maryland	.531	11	Delaware	.647
12	Michigan	.464	12	Illinois	.622
13	Hawaii	.439	13	Washington	.615
14	Idaho	.417	14	Michigan	.594
15	Washington	.406	15	Hawaii	.476
16	Maine	.311	16	Rhode Island	.380
17	Florida	.307	17	Iowa	.376
18	North Dakota	.297	18	Minnesota	.342
19	Alaska	.234	19	North Dakota	.339
20	Utah	.228	20	Wisconsin	.314
21	Minnesota	.227	21	Wyoming	.297
22	New Mexico	.204	22	Nevada	.269
23	Tennessee	.203	23	North Carolina	.260
24	California	.202	24	West Virginia	.200
25	North Carolina	.194	25	Maine	.199
26	Wisconsin	.175	26	Idaho	.176
27	Iowa	.132	27	Virginia	.123
28	Oregon	.051	28	Colorado	.111
29	Vermont	−.045	29	Oregon	.101
30	Arizona	−.051	30	Tennessee	.049
31	Colorado	−.063	31	New Hampshire	−.015
32	Virginia	−.072	32	South Carolina	−.058
33	West Virginia	−.099	33	South Dakota	−.121
34	South Dakota	−.109	34	Alaska	−.184
35	Wyoming	−.125	35	Montana	−.217
36	South Carolina	−.131	36	Kansas	−.230
37	Missouri	−.145	37	Oklahoma	−.252
38	Massachusetts	−.150	38	Massachusetts	−.309
39	Montana	−.155	39	Mississippi	−.318
40	Oklahoma	−.341	40	Arkansas	−.325
41	Kentucky	−.354	41	Texas	−.423

TABLE 3.8 *(continued)*

	DEMOCRATS			REPUBLICANS	
Rank	*State*	*Strength*	*Rank*	*State*	*Strength*
42	Nevada	−.493	42	Missouri	−.425
43	Alabama	−.574	43	Utah	−.433
44	Arkansas	−.579	44	Nebraska	−.495
45	Kansas	−.598	45	Vermont	−.576
46	Georgia	−.626	46	Louisiana	−.607
47	Mississippi	−.671	47	Alabama	−.621
48	Texas	−.717	48	Kentucky	−.696
49	Nebraska	−.819	49	Florida	−.758
50	Louisiana	−.871	50	Georgia	−1.457

Note: See Table C.1 for Ns.

county-level party organizations. Fortunately, comparison of county party units covered in our Party Transformation Study (PTS) survey can be made to the county parties responding to a 1964 survey by the University of Michigan Center for Political Studies (reported by Beck, 1974). There are 122 counties common to the two studies. The advantages of focusing on the CPS study are that it represents a national probability sample, thus allowing generalization; and the data are available for the individual county-level organizations, thus permitting conclusions about change that are not subject to sampling error or to the ecological fallacy. The number of attributes that can be compared is not great, but fortunately the variables available are important components of our party organizational strength concept. Univariate frequencies on these variables are shown in Table 3.9, which reports data for all county parties in the CPS survey, all county parties in our 1979 (PTS) study, and for county parties common to both surveys.[6]

Table 3.9 shows that the CPS county parties represented in our survey differ insignificantly from the total CPS sample of county parties. Comparison of columns 2 and 3 of Table 3.9, which present data on counties common to the two surveys, makes obvious that the party organizations of 1979 were substantially more active than their predecessors in 1964. Each type of activity is more prevalent in 1979 than in 1964, and though in 1964 a clear majority of the parties performed each of the five activities, in 1979 these levels of performance had risen significantly.

A better indication of the nature of change in the performance of these activities can be gained through examination of the cross-tabulation of the activity variables for the two years 1964 and 1979, shown in Table 3.10. For every activity, the modal pattern is one of no change, with a majority of the party organizations performing four of the five activities in both 1964 and

TABLE 3.9.
Change in Attributes of County-level Party Organizations, 1964–1979.

	Column 1 All CPS	Column 2 CPS/PTS	Column 3 PTS/CPS	Column 4 All PTS
	County Parties (1964)	County Parties (1964)	County Parties (1979)	County Parties (1979)
Distribution of campaign literature	80.8[a]	77.6[b]	93.4[c]	78.6[d]
Arrange affairs/ campaign events	63.2	63.7	84.4	66.2
Raise money	59.0	63.2	86.1	69.5
Publicize party & candidate activity	62.0	61.4	62.3	63.7
Registration drives	60.3	64.0	76.2	50.5

[a]For CPS county parties, percent of county parties in which function was well done (in contrast to "not so well done" or "which should be improved in the next campaign"). $N > 208$.

[b]$N > 110$.

[c]For PTS county parties, percent of county parties in which activity was performed. $N > 121$.

[d]$N > 3974$.

Note: CPS refers to county parties included in the Center for Political Studies, University of Michigan, study of 1964 (reported by Beck, 1974). PTS refers to the 1979 survey of the universe of county-level parties as part of the Party Transformation Study (reported in this book).

TABLE 3.10.
Change in Activity Levels of County Party Organizations, 1964–1979.

Activity	Column 1 Performing activity in both years	Column 2 Performing activity in 1964 only	Column 3 Performing activity in 1979 only	Column 4 Performing activity in neither year
Distribute literature	73.3	4.3	20.7	1.7
Arrange events	54.9	8.8	28.3	8.0
Raise money	54.4	8.8	32.5	4.4
Publicity	41.2	20.2	23.7	14.9
Registration drives	51.4	12.6	24.3	11.7

Note: Rows total to 100 percent, except for rounding error. $N > 110$.

TABLE 3.11.
Change in Attributes of Precinct-level Organizations, 1964–1979.

	Column 1 All CPS County Parties (1964)	Column 2 CPS/PTS County Parties (1964)	Column 3 PTS/CPS County Parties (1979)	Column 4 All PTS County Parties (1979)
Percent of precincts with chair				
Mean	79.9	84.1	79.8	78.9
Median	90.0	94.6	85.3	90.2
Precent of precincts with effective chairs				
Mean	54.8	56.8	—	—
Median	50.4	55.0	—	—
Percent of precincts effective at getting out the vote				
Mean	—	—	53.2	54.8
Median	—	—	50.3	50.4
Percent of precincts maintaining lists				
Mean	—	—	76.9	71.6
Median	—	—	99.1	99.5

1979. The second column of the table reports the percentage of county parties performing the activity in 1964, but not in 1979. For each activity there is a larger percentage increase than decrease in the county parties engaging in the activity in the later year (columns 3 and 2 respectively). A small number of county parties was inactive in both years. Thus, we many conclude that to the extent that there is change in levels of party organization activity over time, it is in the direction of more active parties.

Similar evidence of change can be adduced from data on the nature of the precinct-level organizations in these counties (see Table 3.11). In 1964, one-half of the chairs reported 90 percent or more of the precincts in their counties had leaders. The comparable figure for all 1979 county parties is also 90 percent. While the questions are not strictly comparable, the 1964 data reveal that approximately one-half of the precinct chairs were rated as effective at getting out the vote, while our data show that a similar percentage was rated effective in 1979. Were effectiveness defined as simply maintaining lists of voters and contributors, the 1979 data would reveal an overwhelming percentage of effective precinct organizations. The minimal conclusion to be drawn from this analysis is that there is no evidence of decline from 1964 to 1979 in the effectiveness of precinct party organizations.

As might be expected, the precinct organizations are somewhat more volatile than the county organizations. Significant party based differences also exist. For most Republican organizations (58 percent), the median percentage of precinct leader positions filled did not change significantly from the early 1960s to late 1970s.[7] The comparable figure for Democratic organizations is 75 percent. Republican organizations are also more likely to have experienced a decline in the percentage of precincts with filled chairs (29 percent versus 19 percent for the Democrats). Overall, however, 81 percent of the Democratic organizations and 71 percent of the Republican organizations are today at least as successful in organizing their precincts as they were in 1964.[8]

One final bit of evidence on the question of change should be considered. In the 1979 survey the county-level organization leaders were asked to evaluate the strength of the party in their county as compared to 5 to 10 years ago. Table 3.12 reports their responses. A small minority of the party leaders report their party has become weaker, while a clear majority believe their party has become stronger. The party based differences are slight. Obviously, these perceptions do not yield definitive answers to the question of change in organizational attributes, but when combined with the evidence from the CPS survey, it appears that county-level organizations at the end of the 1970s were at least as strong as in the early 1960s.

Conclusions

There is less known about local party organizations and activities than almost any other area of American political institutions. This paucity of data and information is a result of the geographic sweep of the thousands of such party organizations, the lack of funding for comparative research, and the largely anecdotal or place-specific research that has been done. Hardly a book on local, rural or city politics has been written that has failed to comment on the lack of basic research in the field. In this study we have been able to generate data covering a broad and representative sweep of local party organizations. Our findings are as follows:

TABLE 3.12.
County-level Leaders' Perceptions of Change in Party Strength.

Change[a]	Democrats	Republicans
	(percent)	
Significantly stronger	26.9	33.1
Somewhat stronger	23.6	24.9
Little change	24.7	20.0
Somewhat weaker	18.0	14.0
Significantly weaker	6.8	8.0
Total	100.0	100.0
(N)	(1646)	(1512)

[a] The question read: There is a lot of speculation these days concerning the state of political parties and their future. From your experience, how would you evaluate the strength of your party in your county compared to 5–10 years ago?

1. Although most local party organizations are not bureaucratically organized, they do sustain a fairly high level of programmatic activity. A significant minority of such organizations conducts some party maintenance activity in non-election periods.
2. The strength of local party organizations varies significantly by region, but not by party. The major organization building efforts of the Republicans, so successful in terms of state party organizations in the south, have not filtered down to the local level.
3. Local party organizational strength is relatively independent of the strength of the state party organizations, despite the fact that state party organizations give substantial quantities of assistance to the local parties. The development of local party organizations may require much more indigenous support than is required at other levels of organization.
4. Local party organizations have not become less active or less organized over the past two decades. These findings do not support the thesis of party decline.

More specifically, this analysis suggests that the strength of party organization may be dependent upon neither the strength of the party-in-the-electorate, nor the strength of the party-in-government. This complicates the party demise thesis since the consequences of change in one component of party must be assessed within the context of possibly dissimilar change for the other components. Reliable assessments and predictions of the condition of the party system cannot be conducted without giving attention to the party organizations.

We have not isolated the causes and the consequences of local party organizational strength in this chapter, but we have demonstrated the need to incorporate party organizations into the analyses of party systems. It is clear that these organizations have not withered away and they do not appear to be in any danger of doing so.

NOTES

1. In most states, leaders of the county party organization were surveyed. But in some states the equivalent level of party is organized on a basis other than county. In Connecticut, Massachusetts, and Rhode Island, town chairs were surveyed; in Alaska and North Dakota, the questionnaires went to district chairs; in Minnesota some districts were treated as equivalent to counties; and in Louisiana, for the Democrats, the respondents were parish chairs while for the Republicans they were the chairs of the parishes or the Political Action Council Districts; in New Hampshire, the Republican recipients of questionnaires were town and county chairs; in Virginia, town and city chairs were surveyed. Miscellaneous other aberrations in organization were also accommodated—e.g., St. Louis City in Missouri.

2. Hawley (1973, p. 17) found that 64.2 percent of 2960 cities of 5000 population used nonpartisan ballots in 1968, and that the incidence of non-partisanship for county offices was higher. He estimated that 85 percent of all school board members were elected on nonpartisan ballots. The discrepancy between levels of local party participation in city and in county-level campaigns undoubtedly is a function of such nonpartisanship, mitigated by the tendency of some parties to be involved with campaigns for nonpartisan offices at both the county and sub-county levels.

3. Of course not all local party activity is necessarily initiated, supported, or carried out solely by the local organization. The chairs report the following joint state-county activity: sharing contributor and member mail lists, 44 percent; joint fund raising, 42 percent; cooperative recruiting or checking of patronage appointments, 40 percent; joint get-out-the-vote drives, 49 percent; and joint registration drives, 35 percent. Moreover, the state organizations provide significant services to many county-level parties, including: legal advice, 41 percent; research, 34 percent; computer services, 29 percent; assistance with candidate recruitment, 25 percent; assistance with financial record keeping, 15 percent; funds for campaign expenses, 11 percent; staff, 8 percent; funds for operating expenses, 6 percent; and office space, 2 percent.

4. These findings are parallel to Sorauf's (1963) finding that in Pennsylvania, Democratic and Republican organizations were highly correlated in strength at the local level. Additionally, he found that organizational strength was associated with population density, which made for a positive relation between organizational strength and electoral success for Democrats, and inverse relation for the Republicans.

5. Counties and cities and towns are considered to be "major" on the basis of three criteria: (1) counties containing more than 40 percent of their states' population; (2) counties responsible for 40 percent or more of their states' Republican or Democratic vote in the 1976 presidential election; and (3) the largest counties which collectively contain 50 percent of the U.S. population.

6. The CPS items are not identical to our items and the reader may wish to consider their exact wording, which is available from the authors. Professor Paul Beck was very kind in sharing details about his analysis with us.

It should also be noted that the summary measure of party organizational strength created for the complete contemporary sample of PTS counties is moderately to strongly related with the four activity variables that are common to the PTS and CPS studies.

7. This conclusion is based on a cross-tabulation of the categorized variable indicating the percentage of precincts with the leadership filled. The categories used are quartiles. Thus, the conclusion that there has been no change means that for 58 percent of the Republican organizations, the quartile did not change.

8. We do not feel very comfortable in pursuing this mode of analysis with the effectiveness items, because our PTS study focused on specific definitions of effectiveness (e.g., ability to get out the vote), whereas the CPS study used an overall characterization of effectiveness. Because the PTS chairs report that almost all of their precinct organizations maintain lists of voters and contributors, the level of this type of effectiveness today is substantially higher than in 1964. However, in terms of the ability to mobilize voters, effectiveness may have declined among both Republican (42 percent) and Democratic (31 percent) organizations.

4

Relationships among Party
Organizations: Party Integration

A concern for parties as organizations naturally leads to examination of individual party units in terms of their organizational attributes and relations with other party units. Thirty years ago, Duverger (1954, p. 40) posed the question "how are the small basic communities ... which agglomerate to constitute the party, linked with one another?" Like Duverger, we visualize vertical and horizontal linkages among party units, but are concerned in this chapter only with vertical relationships.

Evidence from the late 1950s through early 1960s (Harmel and Janda, 1982) confirms the impression conveyed by Samuel Eldersveld's study of the Wayne County parties (Eldersveld, 1964) that American political parties are among the most decentralized in the world. V. O. Key touched upon this quality of the American parties when he wrote (Key, 1958, p. 346) that "although the party organization can be regarded as a hierarchy ... it may be more accurately described as a system of layers of organization." Then Eldersveld (1964; 1982, p. 99) adapted the term stratarchy to refer to the layered attributes of the party organizations:

> ... an organization with layers, or strata, of control rather than one of
> centralized leadership from the top down.... The party develops this
> pattern of relationships—stratarchical rather than hierarchical—because
> of the necessities of collaborating with and recognizing local echelons for
> votes, money, personnel.

But neither hierarchy nor stratarchy alone suffices to depict the ways in which the party organizations are linked. The era of Democratic party reform has demonstrated the capacity of a national party organization to enforce sanctioned norms against state party organizations. And recent studies have pointed to a "nationalizing" trend for both parties, characterized by tighter integration between the national and state parties (Longley, 1978; Cotter and Bibby, 1980; Jackson and Hitlin, 1981; Huckshorn, et al., 1982). New patterns of integrative relationships have also been stimulated by the Federal Election Campaign Acts of the 1970s.[1]

To examine the patterns of relationship between party units in such a mixed and changing system, it is useful, indeed it may be necessary, to dispense with the alternatives of stratarchy and hierarchy. This can be accomplished by considering patterns of integration within the party system, particularly if integration is thought of in terms of the interdependence of different levels of party organization. The trend toward greater inter-dependence between state party organizations and those at the national and local levels has not been the subject of systematic, cross-sectional study. In this chapter, we present analysis of data on integration collected for parties in the 27 sample states during 1979–1980.

National Party–State Party Integration

Integration involves a pattern of interaction between party units at varying levels and in this instance, between the state and national party organizations. Members of the national party committees, whether holding office ex officio or by virtue of choice by the Republican national convention delegations or through a variety of Democratic state and national party processes, play a role in communicating between the national and state levels of party. Under the rules of some state parties, the national committee members are ex officio state party officers. Gradually since 1952 and culminating in 1968–1972, the parties have incorporated the state chairs as members of the national committees. Today the state chairs, in their dual roles as head of the state party organization and as voting members and a separate caucus within the national committee, have become the principal link between the state and national party organizations.[2]

In consequence of this duality of roles, we have developed measures of state party involvement in national committee affairs, and of national party involvement in state party affairs, based upon the state chairs' responses to questions put to them in interviews.[3] We sought information concerning the principal activities of the state chairs as members of their national committees, the types of state party matters dealt with at the national committee level (with national chairpeople and staff), and the types of state party activities implemented as a result of national committee recom-mendations and financial support.

The degree of state chair involvement in national committee affairs (membership or leadership roles on major committees are the most frequent activity references) and the frequency and range of chairs' dealings with the

TABLE 4.1.
State Party Involvement in National Committee Affairs.

	Republicans		Democrats	
Level of Involvement	N	%	N	%
High	6	22.2	6	24.0
Medium	6	22.2	3	12.0
Low	15	55.6	16	64.0
Total	27	100.0	25	100.0

TABLE 4.2.
National Committee Services to State Party Organizations.

	Percent Receiving Service	
Service	Republicans	Democrats
Staff	63.0	3.8*
Polls and Research	44.4	7.7*
Voter Identification	22.2	19.2
Campaign Seminars	88.9	40.7
Rule Enforcement	0.0	53.8*
Technical Assistance	22.2	22.2
Cash Transfers	51.9	7.4*

*Difference between parties is statistically significant at $p < .05$.

national committee on state party matters were ranked on a trichotomous scale. A majority of state parties (60 percent) ranked low on this measure, though nearly one-fourth were highly involved (Table 4.1). Party differences in levels of involvement were minimal.

The obverse to state chair involvement in national committee affairs is the national party's efforts to influence the organization and processes of the state parties. While there are many subtle forms of such influence, the national committees are most influential when they provide services to the state party organizations. The state party leaders reported receiving six types of services (Table 4.2), in addition to dealing with the national committees on rule enforcement.[4] The service most frequently received by Republican state party organizations is assistance with campaign seminars, while Democrats are most likely to relate to the national committee on matters of rule enforcement. As might be expected, the RNC is much more active than the DNC in supporting its state parties. For instance, the RNC was reported to have provided staff, reflecting a high level of integration, to nearly two-thirds of the state party organization, while only a single Democratic organization reported such support. Moreover, distinctive patterns of support are observed, with the RNC emphasizing service relations and the DNC emphasizing rule enforcement.

These modes of interaction have been combined to form a summary index measure of national party involvement in state party affairs. Because staff, money, and rule enforcement reflect a more dependent position on the part of the state party, these items have been weighted somewhat more heavily in constructing the index. Not surprisingly, Republican state party organizations score substantially higher on the index, receiving on the average 4.1 services (of the 6) compared to the Democratic average of 2.2.

Distinct party differences are observed in the relationship between the indicators of state involvement in national party affairs and national party involvement in state party affairs. For Republican organizations, the relationship is effectively zero ($r = .11$), suggesting that participation in national committee affairs is not a prerequisite to receipt of national party services. For Democratic organizations, a moderate, positive relationship exists ($r = .38$); greater state involvement in national party affairs is associated with greater national party involvement in state party affairs. We will have more to say about these party differences later. These two indicators of integration are the major independent variables in the analysis that follows.

Analysis of National-State Party Integration

The hypothesis that state party organizational strength is in part a function of levels of state party integration with the national party, reflects two major assumptions. The first is that state party organizations will be responsive to national party leadership. The second is that it is quite difficult for party organizations to acquire strength without an infusion of resources. While the initiative for strengthening the party organization may derive from internal sources, from the national committee, from interest groups, or officeholders, parties can rarely acquire strength without the intervention of external forces. Thus, a positive correlation between state party organizational strength and the two dimensions of integration is expected.

A modest correlation between the two variables is observed when current strength[5] is associated with current levels of national-state party integration. For Democrats and Republicans there is a weak tendency for stronger state parties to be more integrated with the national party. Somewhat surprisingly, however, the correlation is a function of only one of the two components of the integration index: greater state party involvement in national party affairs is associated with greater Democratic ($r = .28$) and Republican ($r = .28$) strength, but national party involvement in state party affairs (as reflected in the provision of services) displays no relationship to state party strength within either party. This correlation may reveal unanticipated aspects of the process of socializing state party leaders, which may be important to party integration. There are two facets to this socialization process. The state chairs are co-opted to national party organizational values when they deal by phone and mail with national party officers and staff, and when they meet with them at national committee meetings. The state chairs also socialize each other in formal seminar arrangements and informal interactions, under the aegis of the national committee meetings. Thus, the national parties may perform an important function in the diffusion of innovations, especially in a period marked by rapid innovation in political technology.

This would also account for the similar impact of interaction for Democratic and Republican organizations. Interaction within a framework of increasingly hierarchical national party-state relations enhances Democratic state party organizational strength. Within the context of more stratarchical relationships, Republican interactions are similarly associated with stronger state party organizations.

Finally, we note the possibility that the unexpectedly emphatic impact on state party organizational strength of the state chairs' involvement in national committee affairs may be related to the recency of state chairs taking on the dual role. While the Republicans admitted most chairs to national committee membership on a formula basis in 1952 and to all of them in 1968, the Democrats did not follow suit until 1972, at which time they also designated the vice-chairs of the state parties as members of the national committee. Thus, the decade prior to the conduct of this study was characterized by enrichment of state chair relations to the national party and to other state chairs. This process of socialization to new and nationalizing roles may have had a rippling impact on the vigor of state party leadership and the standards which the chairs set for state party organizations.[6]

This result was not precisely contemplated by the hypothesis. And, indeed, a better test is one correlating integration with change in strength: integration at time t should be associated with increases in strength from t to $t + 1$. But even a further qualification is necessary because it should not be expected that integration would have equivalent impact on weak and strong parties alike. Strong parties would not necessarily benefit from integration to the same degree as weak parties, thus a control for prior levels of strength must also be implemented.

Once change is considered, however, it becomes necessary to control for other variables that might be responsible for the change. For instance, the hypothesis might be recast to assert the expectation that integration at time t should be associated with increases in strength from t to $t + 1$ beyond that which would have been expected to result from the operation of these other variables. Though we are limited by the small number of cases, controls can be implemented for levels of electoral success of the party and for demographic attributes of the states, as possible determinants of change in state party organizational strength.

Two indicators of electoral success are employed: The first is the Democratic share of the two party vote for governor, averaged for elections between 1975 and 1980. The second is change in Austin Ranney's aggregate measure of Democratic electoral success for state offices, from the period 1963–1973 to that of 1974–1980.[7] Demographic variables include median income as an indicator of the wealth of the state, and the percentage of the work force which is unionized. Thus, counting prior levels of strength and state involvement in national party affairs, six independent variables are used to predict current levels of state party organizational strength. The results of this analysis are shown in Table 4.3.

The data reveal that current Republican organization strength is unrelated to all of the independent variables except prior levels of strength. For Democratic organizations a different picture emerges. Current strength is not well predicted in general, although three variables are modestly related to it. Democratic party organizations are strongest in states in which the Democrats have been most successful electorally, in relatively wealthy states, and in states in which the state party is integrated with the national organization. Interestingly, integration itself is unrelated to the other predictors, thus substantial party differences exist.

Our data are not adequate to conduct the most thorough test of the hypothesis, largely due to the difficulty of collecting longitudinal data. However, it is possible to consider the problem of controlling for prior levels of state organizational strength, and these data are shown in Fig. 4.1. The direction of causality between integration$_t$ and organizational strength$_t$ is not depicted because when measured at the same point in time, integration may cause strength (the preferred hypothesis), strength may cause integration, or there may be reciprocal causation. Moreover, the stability of the analysis is limited by the small number of cases. Nonetheless, some suggestive patterns emerge. For Democratic organizations, current levels of strength reflect to a limited degree state party involvement in national party affairs ($r = .28$), which in turn is strongly associated with prior strength (the strongest parties of the early 1970s interacting most with the national party in the late 1970s). But current levels of strength are independent of prior levels of strength ($r = .13$). Levels of service or rule enforcement interaction bear no relationship to either current or previous levels of organizational strength. Moreover, change in strength is unrelated to the service indicator, although

TABLE 4.3.
Determinants of Party Organizational Strength.

	Democrats			Republicans		
	Cumulative R^2	Beta	r	Cumulative R^2	Beta	r
Organizational strength$_{t-1}$	.018	−.252	.134	.778	.905	.882
Gubernatorial vote	.031	.149	.064	.782	.079	−.270
Change in electoral success	.129	.353	.336	.813	.269	.320
% of workforce which is unionized	.183	−.152	.045	.825	−.136	.201
Median income	.245	.353	.382	.826	−.012	.306
State party involvement in national party affairs	.341	.417	.283	.826	−.021	.279
Final R^2	.341			.864		
Adjusted R^2	−.450			.661		
N	12-27			16-27		

DEMOCRATS

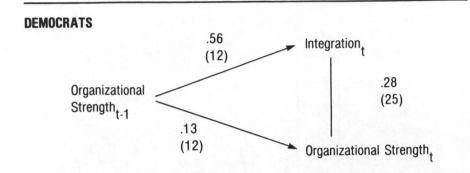

REPUBLICANS

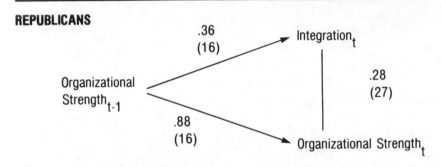

Note: Integration is indicated by the degree of state party involvement in national party affairs.

FIGURE 4.1. State Party Strength and Integration with the National Party.

there is some tendency for involvement in national party affairs to be associated with decreases in strength ($r = -.35$) from the early 1970s to the late 1970s.

For Republican organizations the pattern is different. Current strength is strongly associated with earlier levels of strength ($r = .88$), suggesting a much more systematic pattern of change for Republican as compared to Democratic organizations. Current strength is only modestly related to levels of involvement in the national party, which are in turn only weakly related to prior levels of strength. Levels of services have no impact on current strength. Change in levels of strength is unrelated to the degree of integration with the national party.

These data provide some significant clues to the processes that are occurring. For the Republican organizations, involvement in, receipt of services from, and integration with the national party have no discernable impact on current state party organizational strength, despite a fairly high level of activity on the part of the RNC. Perhaps RNC state party-building efforts in the 1960s were attended by such success that national party-state integration can no longer add measurable increments to the resultant high levels of Republican state party strength. Current RNC activity may contribute to organizational maintenance, rather than organization building, and may be directed toward weaker and stronger parties alike. The marginal costs of strengthening already strong organizations may also be quite high, as is the cost of strengthening weak organizations which have resisted such party building efforts in the past. If the impact of national party effort was to counter the party eroding forces in the changing political environment, we would not expect to find strong relationships between measures of party integration and change in state party organizational strength over time. Finally, the strong correlation for earlier and later state Republican party strength is evidence of the success of these party organizations in maintaining organizational continuity. Perhaps in some large measure the service efforts of the RNC are responsive to the capacities of strong party organizations to use, and hence to provide a sustained demand for such services.

The process is quite different within the Democratic party, where the process reflects the much lower organizational strength of Democratic state organizations. These organizations have strengthened over the past two decades but few have come close to the level of organizational strength of the Republican state organizations. Consequently, national party effort can have some impact, both in terms of maintaining the stronger party organizations, and strengthening weaker state organizations. But, as Tables 4.4 and 4.5 demonstrate, the DNC accomplished this despite a diminution of service activity over the last two decades. This finding merely reinforces our earlier interpretation that through the promulgation of norms favorable to organizational development, the DNC provides the incentives for strengthening organizations, and by providing a forum for the exchange of information the means of development are made known. National party material resources thus do not seem to be crucial to state party organizational strength.

It has been suggested (Cotter and Bibby, 1980) that the RNC approach to integrative relationships with the state party organizations has been to emphasize service, whereas the DNC approach has been to emphasize rulemaking, adjudication, and hierarchical relations. These patterns are confirmed in Tables 4.1 and 4.2. Many scholars have expected that the service emphasis would strengthen and that the rules reform emphasis would weaken the state party organizations. The present analysis does not confirm those expectations. The weaker of the two national party organizations, the DNC, with its emphasis upon rules and hierarchical relationships, appears to have a measurably greater impact upon the strength of state parties than does the service-oriented and stronger RNC. Our analysis neither confirms nor disconfirms the expectation that national party rules emphasis is associated

TABLE 4.4.
State Party Interactions with the National Committees, 1960–1980.

| | Percent Interacting Regularly | | | | | | | | Percent Never Interacting | | | | | | | |
| | Republicans | | | | Democrats | | | | Republicans | | | | Democrats | | | |
	1960–1964	1965–1969	1970–1974	1975–1980	1960–1964	1965–1969	1970–1974	1975–1980	1960–1964	1965–1969	1970–1974	1975–1980	1960–1964	1965–1969	1970–1974	1975–1980
On federal appointments	33.3	35.5	34.8	32.7	40.0	34.8	7.7	8.8	28.6	38.7	13.0	21.2	13.3	21.7	53.8	55.9
On speakers	52.4	60.6	53.2	58.5	62.5	27.3	29.6	13.9	0.0	3.0	2.1	3.8	0.0	9.1	11.1	16.7
On candidate assistance	35.3	34.4	24.4	43.1	20.0	19.0	20.0	5.9	11.8	18.8	28.9	17.6	6.7	23.8	44.0	55.9
On fund-raising	45.0	46.9	34.8	37.3	42.9	30.4	30.8	8.3	5.0	12.5	8.7	3.9	14.3	17.4	19.2	16.7
On national convention matters	55.0	43.8	44.2	59.2	40.0	60.0	47.8	36.1	10.0	6.3	11.6	6.1	6.7	15.0	4.3	2.8
N	16	30	43	46	13	19	23	32	16	30	43	46	13	19	23	32

TABLE 4.5.
Average State Party Interactions with the National Committee, 1960–1980

Frequency of Interaction	Republicans					Democrats				
	1960–1964	1965–1969	1970–1974	1975–1980		1960–1964	1965–1969	1970–1974	1975–1980
Mean	8.7	8.5	8.7	8.2		8.7	9.3	9.9	10.8
N	16	30	43	46		13	19	23	32

Note: Low scores indicate greater frequency of interaction.

with weak state parties, because the fruits of state chair participation in the affairs of the national party are not mitigated by the DNC's rules emphasis or enhanced by the RNC's service emphasis. The second consideration is that state Democratic parties are sufficiently weak that small influences stemming from a relationship to the national party may be magnified in their impact, and the state Republican parties are so comparatively strong that national party impact can be absorbed without measurable change in organizational strength.

Perhaps the most significant implication of all this is that state party organizations can be maintained and increased in their organizational strength through elements of their association with the national party organization, and in the apparent absence of supporting trends in the other components of party: the party-in-the-electorate and the party-in-government. Indeed, we speculate that even the so-called "anti-party" mood of the electorate, a mood which is perhaps better characterized as neutrality toward rather than opposition to the parties, may not significantly undermine the party organizations in the short run (see Wattenberg, 1981). As the state and national parties become more closely integrated, party resources can be diverted toward organization maintenance in areas of the country in which the electoral fortunes of the party are dragging. In this sense, parties become nationalized, and state party organizations become less dependent upon short-term perturbations in the local electoral system.

State Party Integration with Local Parties as Determinant of Local Party Organizational Strength

Interdependence between the state and local parties, just as between the state and national parties, implies joint activity toward common goals, or it implies a process of reciprocity in which the party organizations at different levels assist each other in achieving their goals. When one level of organization consistently exploits another for its own purposes, such an asymmetrical relationship cannot be considered interdependent. Instead, integration implies commonality and reciprocity.

"Degree of integration" is taken to be an attribute of each local party organization. Consequently, a measure of integration for each of the local parties has been constructed from the questionnaire responses of the local party leaders. State-local party integration consists of six subdimensions:

1. the legal relationship of state and local parties;
2. the degree of structural integration of state and local parties;
3. the level of communication between organizations;
4. state party support for local party activity;

TABLE 4.6.
Indicators of State-local Party Integration (County-level Data).

Indicator	Democrats	Republicans
Percent reporting that state party must clear some local party actions	17.8	15.9
Percent members of state committee	32.8	35.5
Percent in contact with state party often throughout the year	37.7	38.8
Percent receiving service—		
legal advice	37.3	44.9
research	26.6	40.4
computer services	24.7	33.1
candidate recruitment	25.3	34.3
financial record keeping	11.0	18.3
campaign expenses	10.1	12.2
staff	7.2	7.9
operating expenses	5.7	5.4
office space	1.5	1.7
no service	32.9	27.3
Percent engaging in joint state-local activity—		
get-out-the-vote	51.0	47.3
mailing lists	39.1	49.1
funding raising	42.3	41.7
patronage	40.8	39.1
registration drives	39.3	30.4
no activity	31.1	32.9
Percent reporting an inconsequential role of state party chair in local chair's recruitment and selection	90.4	87.6

Democratic $N > 1683$; Republican $N > 1505$.

5. joint state-local programs;
6. state party involvement in the selection of local leaders.

Summary data on each of the six variables are shown in Table 4.6. An index of party integration was computed from these six measures. The variables are moderately intercorrelated and consequently reveal a unidimensional structure when factor analyzed. These items can be used to calculate a measure of party integration, with a range of 0 to 60, a mean of 20.4, and a standard deviation of 12.2. Less than 10 percent of the parties score 40 or above on the measure, but only 3 percent have a score of 0. Little party-related variability in the index is apparent, with Republican county organizations scoring significantly (statistically) but only slightly higher than Democratic organizations.

There is only a moderate tendency for stronger local parties to be better integrated with their state parties. Still, using the local party as the unit of analysis, the correlation between local organizational strength and integration is .37.

Analysis of State-Local Party Integration

The strength of party organizations at one level may be relevant to the strength of party organizations with which they relate at another level. And party integration may be a function of strength and may be a determinant of strength. At the national-state level of integration, we have found that some state party organizations are strengthened through their relations with the national party committees.

Employing data on 53 state parties and county-level parties in the 27 sample states, we now explore the relationship between strength and integration at this level. We expect an interactive relationship between strength at the state and county levels, and between integration and strength.

The hypotheses to be considered are:

H1: Levels of state-local party integration are a function of the levels of organizational strength of both the state and local party organizations.

H2: Levels of local organizational strength are a function of both state party strength and levels of state-local party integration.

H3: Levels of state organizational strength are a function of both local party strength and levels of state-local party integration.

Integration as Function of State and Local Party Strength

In order for a state party to devote resources to the development and maintenance of local organizations, it must itself have a minimal level of strength. A state party struggling to maintain its own headquarters cannot be expected to concern itself with the condition of local party organizations. Thus, the first hypothesis (H1) is that levels of state party integration are a function of the level of strength of the state party organizations.

Fig. 4.2 reports the data relevant to the hypothesis. For both Republican and Democratic parties the relationship is curvilinear, although for neither party is it very strong. Inspection of the Democratic scattergram reveals that

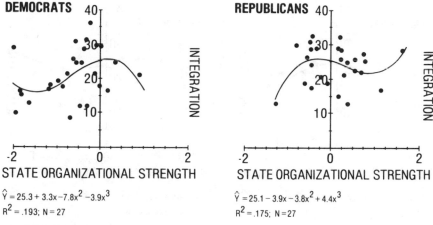

FIGURE 4.2. State-local Party Integration in Relation to State Party Organizational Strength.

greater state organizational strength to a certain extent is associated with greater integration with local parties. At a score of roughly −.75 on the organizational strength index there seems to be a bifurcation, with increments in strength being associated with increases in integration for some parties, but not for others. This may reflect nothing more than alternative strategic decisions on the part of the state Democratic parties. In some states, the party may believe its goals are best achieved through state-level effort and activity, especially where local parties are moribund, while in other states the preferred avenue of activity is through the local parties. It is clear that for the Democrats, increments in state strength do not directly result in increments in local party integration.

The Republican pattern is somewhat different, although it should be remembered that many more Republican than Democratic state organizations are relatively high in strength and conversely fewer are low in strength. The Republican data are compatible with a three-stage pattern of organizational development. When the state party is relatively weak, increments in strength seem to be associated with increments in integration. Here the strategy seems to be one of simultaneously developing state and local party organizations. However, for state parties of intermediate strength, increments in strength are not associated with increments in integration, suggesting the diversion of state party resources to other purposes. At relatively high levels of strength the pattern changes again. Perhaps only as state party organizations become secure in their own strength are they willing to siphon off resources and effort towards relating with the local parties.[8] Later we shall explore this developmental pattern in greater detail, but at

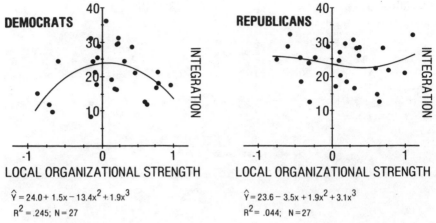

$$\hat{Y} = 24.0 + 1.5x - 13.4x^2 + 1.9x^3$$
$$R^2 = .245; \quad N = 27$$

$$\hat{Y} = 23.6 - 3.5x + 1.9x^2 + 3.1x^3$$
$$R^2 = .044; \quad N = 27$$

FIGURE 4.3. State-local 'Party Integration in Relation to Local Party Organizational Strength.

present two caveats must be expressed. First, the amount of variance explained is not particularly high for either party. Second, the curves are somewhat difficult to interpret at the extreme points because of the relatively small number of parties. Thus, caution in these interpretations is essential.

It may also be hypothesized (again, H1) that party integration is in part a function of the strength of the local party organizations. Here we clearly expect that relationship to be curvilinear: where local organizations are weak, integration is expected to be slight because little organization exists to be integrated. However, integration may also be low where the local organizations are relatively strong. Strong local parties are likely to resist efforts by the state party to constrain their activity and discretion, and are less likely to need to rely on the resources of the state party. Indeed, a local party of sufficient strength may dominate the state party—hardly a relationship of interdependence. The Cook County Democratic Party, for example, finds it convenient to control the Illinois State Democratic Central Committee, but would have little incentive to deal with it as an equal. The expected form of the curvilinear relationship of local strength and integration is then that of a convex quadratic function. Fig. 4.3 reports the relevant data.

The hypothesis that local party strength is associated with levels of party integration is strongly supported for the Democrats, but completely unsupported for the Republicans. Integration is highest in those states in which the local Democratic party organizations are neither too strong, nor too weak, satisfying our curvilinear expectation. Strong local Democratic parties seem

TABLE 4.7
A Multivariate Analysis of State-local Party Integration

Variable	Unstandardized Regression Coefficients
state party strength	−5.6
state party strength-squared	−5.3[c]
state party strength-cubed	6.1[c]
local party strength	−5.9
local party strength-squared	5.9
party[a]	1.5
south[b]	5.7[c]
party-state party strength	9.0
party-state party strength-squared	−2.4
party-state party strength-cubed	−10.4[c]
party-local party strength	6.1
party-local party strength-squared	−13.9[c]
R^2	.41[c]
$\bar{R}^2$	.23
N	54
intercept	20.7

[a]Party: 0 = Republican; 1 = Democrat
[b]South: 0 = South; 1 = non-South
[c]$p < .05$.

to be incompatible with high levels of party integration. For the Republicans, no such relationship exists: in states in which the Republican county organizations are strong, integration is neither helped nor harmed.[9]

Table 4.7 reports the results of a multivariate analysis of party integration scores. The equation is relatively complex, including curvilinear terms for state and local strength, interaction terms for strength and party, and a dummy South-non-South variable. Overall, the equation provides a relatively good fit to the data ($R^2 = .405$, significant at .05). The equation can be manipulated to reveal that levels of integration within Republican parties are largely a function of variability in the strength of state party organizations, whereas levels of integration within Democratic parties are largely a function of variability in the strength of local party organizations. Generally, Republican party integration is maximized when the state party organizations are very strong. Democratic party integration is maximized when the local parties are moderately strong.

Local Party Strength as a Function of State Party Strength and Integration

In theory, the strength of either or both levels of party organization may have an impact upon the patterns of relationship between state and local party organizations. The broader jurisdiction of the state party and its presumed advantage in resources, makes it plausible to think in terms of state party strength together with party integration contributing to the development of local party organizational strength (H2). If there is a relationship between local and state strength in the absence of a relationship between strength and integration, we will consider the state-local relationship as spurious, on the assumption that some exogenous variable causes both state and local strength. Thus, the hypothesis to be tested is that local party organizational strength is a function of state party strength and levels of state-local party integration.

There is little support for this hypothesis. Even allowing for curvilinear relationships, only 12.9 percent of the across state variance in average Republican local party organizational strength is accounted for by the state party strength and average state-local integration variables. Although the figure for the Democrats is 22.8 percent and therefore stronger than in the case of the Republicans, this is primarily due to the influence of state party organizational strength. Thus the relationship is probably spurious. The analysis makes it difficult to conclude that the Republican and Democratic state committees bear some responsibility for the condition of the local parties.

State Party Strength as a Function of Local Party Strength and Integration

A somewhat less obvious hypothesis is that state party organizational strength is a function of local party strength and levels of party integration (H3). While it may be less intuitively pleasing to assume strong local party organizations will create strong state party organizations, it is conceivable that once local parties reach a threshold of strength they will find it in their interest to build a strong state party organization. Below this threshold level of strength, competition between state and local parties for resources may deter local party leaders from assisting in the creation of a strong state party. Again, as a hedge against spurious relationships, we will require that local strength and levels of integration each contribute to the explanation of state party strength.

Only modest support for the hypothesis is found for the Democrats. Democratic state party organizations are stronger where local party organizations are stronger ($R^2 = .156$), but party integration adds only marginally to the explanation of state strength ($R^2 = .203$). For the Republicans, however, the hypothesis receives more support. Local strength (in a cubic relationship) accounts for 14.3 percent of the variance in state party strength where levels of party integration increase (in a quadratic equation) R^2 to .254. This still is not a strong relationship, but it suggests that local party organizations may have had a role in the development of strong state party organizations among Republicans.

Cross-Party Strength Relationships

At several points we have argued that organizational development by one party, typically the Republicans because of their history of electoral subordination and because of their penchant for organization as a means of improving their competitive position, stimulates organizational development by the opposition. We can provide a test, albeit a rather limited one, of this proposition. Within each of the time periods used in our analysis, the Republican and Democratic party organizational strength scores have been correlated, with the following results:

	1960–1964	1965–1969	1970–1974	1975–1980
r	.75 (6)	.95 (8)	.52 (15)	.35 (41)

Missing data and the small number of cases make these correlations somewhat suspect, but it does seem that in all time periods there is some relationship between the strength of the Republican and Democratic state party organizations. This tendency is considerably stronger in the 1960s than in the 1970s. It is conceivable that a portion of the decline in the correlation is due to the efforts of the RNC to build strong party organizations. In the past, party organizations developed largely in response to indigenous factors, and consequently the Republicans and Democrats developed simultaneously or interactively. However, in the 1970s the RNC intervened in states— particularly the South—stimulating such significant development that it could not be matched by the Democrats. Thus, the degree of co-variance between the organizational strength of the two parties weakened.

Nonetheless, there is still some evidence that the two parties stimulate each other to organizational development. For 18 states, we have organizational strength scores for at least one point in the 1960s and one point in the 1970s for both parties. For these states, the correlation between change in organizational strength for the Democrats and Republicans is .30, suggesting that where the Republicans have increased in strength so have the Democrats. Of course, this could be due to factors in the environments of the states causing both parties to develop organizationally independently of one another, although we doubt that explanation.

Finally, we should note that there is considerable continuity in strength within both parties. For the 24 Democratic organizations for which data are available for the two decades, the correlation is .64 while for the 33 Republican organizations the correlation is .51. Thus, though there is slightly less continuity for the Republicans, strength in the 1970s was still to a significant degree a function of strength in the 1960s.

Conclusion

In this chapter we have used the concept of integration (inter-dependence) to explore party inter-organizational relationships. The patterns of interaction between the national Democratic and Republican parties with their state affiliates are quite different. The DNC emphasized rule enforcement and the RNC stressed the provision of services, making it clear that state party organizational strength benefits from their association with the national committees, even in an era which has been characterized as having significant anti-party forces at work.

Distinct party differences emerged in the analysis of integration of state and local party organizations. Levels of integration within the Republican parties were largely a function of the variability in the strength of state organizations. By contrast, for the Democratic party, differing levels of integration were most strongly related to the strength of local party organizations. Republican integration is fostered by strong state organizations while Democratic party integration is maximized when local parties are strong.

NOTES

1. These patterns are partially documented in U.S. Supreme Court decisions. At the national level, both the Democrats and Republicans secured Federal Election Commission assent that the campaign committees in the Senate act as agents for the national party committees for purposes of using the DNC and RNC legal expenditure entitlements for senatorial campaigns, thus heralding a new relationship between the national committees and the congressional committees, which have traditionally been competitive and even jealous. This means of enhancing its legal expenditure power by serving as agent for another party committee proved so attractive to the National Republican Senatorial Campaign Committee that it entered into similar agreements with Republican state committees, thus creating specific functional linkages between the "presidential," the "congressional," and the state party organizations. When the Democratic Senatorial Campaign Committee challenged FEC approval of this

arrangement in the courts, the Supreme Court on appeal approved the FEC interpretation of the governing Federal Election Campaign Acts. (See *Federal Election Commission* v. *Democratic Senatorial Campaign Committee*, 454 U.S. 27 (1981).) Furthermore, the Supreme Court inferentially validated the claim of the national party that it can legislate for state parties on matters pertaining to presidential nominating conventions. Illinois and Wisconsin Democrats sought to invoke the provisions of state law and the jurisdiction of state courts to exempt the state parties from national party rules concerning delegate selection. In decisions which are celebrated as establishing the superiority of national party rules over contrary state law pertaining to selecting delegates to presidential nominating conventions, the U.S. Supreme Court also sustained the national party authority over the state parties, an authority sanctioned by the power to refuse to seat delegates. (See *Cousins* v. *Wigoda*, 419 U.S. 477 (1975); and *Democratic Party of United States* v. *La Follette*, 450 U.S. 107 (1981).)

2. Since 1952 most of the chairs of the Republican state parties (on application of a formula keyed to electoral successes) have been members of the RNC and since 1968 all of them have. In 1972, the Democrats acted to make their state chairs and next highest ranking state party officer of opposite sex members of the DNC. For a full report on this effort see Huckshorn (1976, pp. 179–87).

3. Of course, a certain amount of measurement error is introduced through reliance on the state party leaders as informants on state party-national party interactions. Since we are trying to characterize each state party on the degree to which it is integrated with the national party, there are few alternatives to this approach. It should also be noted that the analysis which follows is based upon the responses of the state chairs in the 53 responding sample state parties, not the universe of 100 state parties. In personal interviews with state chairs, they were asked about attendance at national committee meetings, and participation in State Chairmen's Association affairs, and were presented with bidirectional questions about direct involvement with the national committee. Because the overwhelming number of chairs of both parties report that they regularly attend national party meetings, and since a significant number of state chairs view the State Chairmen's Association as a vehicle for pursuing interests discrete from, if not antagonistic to the interests of the national committee, these items were not deemed suitable measures of our concept of integration.

4. Measurement error may be especially severe here because we are asking the state chairs, not the national chairs, to report on the amount of national influence over the state party. No doubt, the state chairs systematically underestimate the degree of influence. On the other hand, to rely on informants from the national party may systematically overestimate the degree of influence.

5. The measure of organizational strength which is employed is the average (across all responses) for the state party for the period 1975–1980. Thus the score is not usually based solely on the response of the state chair who provides information about the degree of integration with the national party.

6. We cannot discount the possibility that the causality flows in the opposite direction. It may be that the leaders of more developed state party organizations are more self-motivated (or more encouraged by the national organizations) to participate in national party affairs. Whatever the process, stronger state party organizations do

interact with the national party more frequently than do weaker party organizations.

7. The measure used was originally constructed by Ranney (1965) and is commonly referred to as a measure of interparty competition. It ranges from a score of 0 (indicating complete Republican domination of the governorship and state legislature) to 1.000 (indicating complete Democratic domination). The actual variable employed is simply the difference between the index score for the period 1974–1980 as reported in Bibby, et al. (1983), and for the period 1963–1973 as shown in Ranney (1976).

8. Given our conceptual definition of integration, the theoretical culmination of this process is not, of course, the merger of state and local parties, but is instead expressed by perfect interdependence.

9. Consistently with this, there is no difference in levels of Republican party integration between the South and the remainder of the country, even though the Republican county parties in the South are substantially weaker than elsewhere.

5

Party Organizations and Electoral Politics: Do Strong Parties Make a Difference?

The measures of state and local party organizational strength developed and applied in Chapters 2 and 3 have intrinsic significance as tests of prevalent perceptions of the condition of the parties as organizations. But they also permit us to assess the instrumental significance of such organizations. In Chapter 4, propositions were tested that concerned the interactive consequences of aspects of party organizational strength for varying strata of party. The present chapter marks a transition from concern for party organizations as ends in themselves, to concern for the middle range consequences of party for the political process. Here we examine the relationship of parties to electoral success, and in Chapter 6 their relationship to linkage with officeholders. In Chapter 7 we assess the impact on party organizations of some aspects of the political environment that commonly are regarded as threats to the parties. In the final chapter, we move to the system level, analyzing the implications of our findings for theories of party and electoral transformation.

Two schools of thought persist on the question of the electoral role of the American parties. One school is associated with Schattschneider's (1948, p. 23) perception of political parties as *"teleological associations of purposeful people,"* that recruit candidates and wage election campaigns towards the end of using government to enact their policies. The second school, associated with Schumpeter (1942) and Downs (1957) emphasizes election winning as an end in itself and treats party concern with policy as incidental to vote winning. As Downs (1957, p. 28) put it, "parties formulate policies in order to win elections, rather than win elections in order to formulate policies." Looking upon party as primarily a vote winning enterprise, in the Downsian tradition, we pose the question whether the strength of the party's organization is relevant to winning votes.

Electoral Success and Interparty Competition

Some of the hypotheses we consider in this chapter are rightly framed as tests of the relationship of party organizational strength (POS) to electoral success. Some have traditionally been put in terms of the relationship of electoral success and of interparty competition to party organizational strength. It is expedient to begin the analysis by considering the nuances which distinguish the meaning of these terms.

Electoral success is conceptualized as the party's share of the vote. In its simplest form, it may be indicated by the percentage of the two-party vote won by the party's candidate for a single office—here the office of governor. If the analysis is to reflect change, it is also necessary to establish patterns of success over time. However, the electoral success measure may take a more complex form, for example, as was proposed by Ranney and Kendall (1954) and further developed by Ranney (1965). Ranney has formulated a compound measure that includes the proportion of votes for the leading statewide office, the proportion of legislative seats won, and takes into account the incidence of control of the governorship and of each house of the legislature, and the incidence of divided government, over time. It is computed in terms of the average percentage of the two-party vote won by Democratic gubernatorial candidates, the average percentage of the seats in the state legislature held by the Democrats, and the proportion of time in which control of the governorship and legislature has been divided between the parties. Ranney scales Democratic electoral success from 0.0 to 1.00, with Republican success computed as the obverse of Democratic success.

The scores computed under the Ranney formula may be treated as continuous measures of the extent to which the electoral politics of a state are dominated by the Democrats or the Republicans. Ranney has also transformed the scale into a categorical measure by inserting breaking points that associate specific ranges of the scale with "one-party Democratic," "modified one-party Democratic," "two party," "modified one-party Republican," and "one-party Republican" patterns of electoral success. These breaking points are generally accepted as delineating five possible kinds of party systems.[1]

Although the Ranney measure is a compound measure of the relative electoral success of state Democratic and Republican parties, it is customarily treated as measuring interparty competition, with the midpoint of the scale denoting the highest level of competitiveness. Conceptually, competitiveness moves beyond the characterization of the relative electoral success of a designated party to identify attributes of a party system that transcend party identification. To transform Ranney's relative electoral success scale into a linear, continuous measure of interparty competition, it is necessary to "fold" the scale at its midpoint. By subtracting .5 from the scores on the relative electoral success scale, and taking the absolute value of the resulting score, a party-neutral measure of interparty competition is created that ranges from 0.0 (indicating perfect competitiveness) to .5 (indicating complete electoral dominance by one party, either Democratic or Republican).

We then have three closely related but conceptually distinguishable measures. Two are party-specific and denote levels of party electoral success. The first of these, gubernatorial electoral success (GES), figures in the analysis of the impact of relative party organizational strength on winning votes for a single office. This is presented in the last part of the chapter. The compound measure of relative electoral success (RES) is employed in its continuous and categorical forms. Together with the "folded" Ranney measure of interparty competitiveness (IPC), the compound measure figures in the analysis that immediately follows.

The analysis in this chapter tests various linkages in the following model:

$$\text{RES/IPC} \rightarrow \text{POS} \rightarrow \text{GES}$$

The introduction of variants of these measures in appropriate contexts will enable us to consider the impact of IPC/RES on change in POS and of the relative strength of party organizations on incremental change in GES.

Strength in Relation to Success and Competitiveness

From the perspective of our robust expectations for the performance of party organizations, the intuitively attractive hypothesis is that POS conduces to electoral success and interparty competition. The criticism directed at the parties for their alleged failure as electoral agents (e.g., Pomper, 1977) suggests that indeed this is the conventional expectation.

But surely reciprocal causation is involved. From the perspective of the "nonparty politics" of the South, Key derived the hypothesis that POS is determined by, rather than determining, the electoral relationship of the parties. He noted that "in states with a normal electoral division hovering around or moving toward the 50-50 point the prospects for a reconstruction of party organization and a vitalization of party competition are better" (Key, 1956, p. 132). We suspect that over time the organizational strength of one party has a reciprocal relationship with relative electoral success and with interparty competition. We also suspect that it is related reciprocally with the strength of the other party in the system (see Chap. 4).[2]

Speculating on how such a process might work, we begin with two organizationally weak parties in an underdeveloped, non-competitive system.

The RES levels of one party would be very high, and in consequence, IPC would be low. The introduction of a stimulus, such as a presidential candidacy of great regional attractiveness, or the intervention of the national party organization, could induce the electorally subordinate party to attempt to improve its capacity to mobilize votes. One means for doing this would be to develop the party organization. From what we now know of the national party committees (Cotter and Bibby, 1980; Bibby, 1979, 1981; Huckshorn, et al., 1982b; Cotter, 1983, pp. 275–78), we would expect that the national party headquarters might invest resources in this kind of organizational effort. Increasing electoral success for the presidential candidate could well provide the incentive to continue with organizational development and to pursue electoral success at state-wide and congressional levels. The changing party image within the electorate might be expected to bring out stronger candidates for office, further enhancing success prospects. Both the organizing efforts and the electoral success experience of the subordinate party would lead to a protective reaction by the traditionally dominant party in increased emphasis on organization and electioneering. Increasing competitiveness within the party system might also provide the incentive to reconcile factional differences and achieve greater cohesion in the nominating processes. In a dynamic model, Key's hypothesis becomes appropriate, with the relationship between RES/IPC and POS becoming reciprocal.

It may well be difficult to track down this dynamic process statistically since electoral tremors that register as minute changes in the relative electoral success and interparty competition scores may bring about equilibrating adjustments to party organizational strength that are of sufficiently low magnitude, delayed in time, or offsetting so as to fail to register statistically.

For example, a close gubernatorial victory could actually dilute the strength of the party organization in the short run (e.g., by imposing a large campaign debt on the party), while simultaneously stimulating the opposition party to organizational effort. And in noncompetitive systems, as Key has suggested, the dominant party will most likely be organizationally weak, while the organizational strength of the subordinate party may be attained prior to any discernible electoral impact. Hence the complex interrelationships may not be easily documented statistically. Moreover, the limitations of our data base make it difficult to test comprehensively the hypothesized dynamic model. Recognizing the limited significance of any findings, we test the following hypotheses:

H1: Relative electoral success and interparty competition at time t and party organizational strength at time t covary.

H2: Those parties with a history of electoral subordination (i.e., that have not been competitive in the past) will be the parties that

TABLE 5.1.
Correlation of Relative Electoral Success and Party Organizational Strength.

Party Organizational Strength	Mean[a]	Relative Electoral Success		
		1946–1963	1962–1972	1974–1980
DEMOCRATS				
1960–1964	−.902	−.79 (13)	−.69 (13)	−.48 (13)
1965–1969	−.022	−.41 (15)	−.26 (15)	−.25 (15)
1970–1974	−.062	−.42 (24)	−.41 (24)	−.25 (24)
1975–1980	−.458	−.17 (45)	−.16 (45)	−.09 (45)
REPUBLICANS				
1960–1964	−.511	−.61 (12)	−.81 (12)	−.76 (12)
1965–1969	.189	−.36 (23)	−.19 (23)	−.22 (23)
1970–1974	.420	−.09 (31)	−.24 (31)	−.15 (31)
1975–1980	.377	−.09 (45)	−.12 (45)	−.04 (45)
Mean		.562	.585	.643

[a]$N = 50$

> demonstrate the greatest amount of change in organizational strength from $t - 1$ to t.
>
> H3: Change in relative electoral success and interparty competition scores over time ($t - 1$ to t) are associated with corresponding changes in party organizational strength.

Do Relative Electoral Success and Interparty Competition Influence Party Organizational Strength?

In the early 1960s there was a strong relationship between RES scores and POS, seeming to confirm Hypothesis 1 (Table 5.1). However, the relationship differs dramatically between the two parties. For Democrats, the strongest organizations were found in those states in which the party had not experienced great electoral success, and the weakest organizations in those states in which the party had its greatest electoral success ($r = -.79$; $N = 13$). This may reflect the peculiar southern experience of the Democrats (although only four of the 13 state parties for which we have organizational data from the early 1960s are from the South). For Republican organizations, the relationship is precisely the opposite ($r = -.61$; $N = 12$): the strongest Republican organizations were to be found in states in which the party was electorally strong (three of the 12 organizations for which we have data are from the South).

By the end of the 1970s, however, there is virtually no relationship between RES and POS for either party with the correlations of strength and success for both parties having declined to nearly zero. Strong Republican and Democratic party organizations are to be found in states in which the parties do well at the polls and in states in which they do not. Success does not appear to strengthen the organizations.

Perhaps this finding is a function of the relative level of organizational strength, especially for the Republicans. When party organizations are relatively weak, as both the Democratic and Republican state parties of the early 1960s were (see the means in Table 5.1), the success-strength relationship may be somewhat stronger. Weak organizations are buffeted more by the changing winds of the electoral climate. As party organizations acquire strength, they become somewhat more insulated from electoral vagaries, in part because the very process of institutionalization is one of making the organization less dependent upon its environment. This same process may apply to the Democrats, but since they have not generally achieved the level of strength of Republican organizations, there may be a slight lag involved. Instead of reacting to electoral tides, the Democratic organizations may be reacting to the organizational development of the Republicans.[3] As the Republicans have acquired sophisticated organizational attributes, the Democrats have been impelled to follow suit, even in the absence of electoral pressures. Over time, the party-as-organization has become somewhat more disjunct from the party-in-the-electorate.

This can be confirmed by the data in Table 5.2, which reports the average organizational strength scores for varying levels of interparty competition (the folded Ranney measure) in the late 1970s. For the Democrats, there is a slight tendency for the non-competitive parties to be organizationally weak, but generally increased competitiveness is not associated with increased strength. For Republicans, as well, there is no meaningful relationship between competitiveness and strength; the differences among the mean organizational strength scores at different levels of competition are inconsequential. The relationship between competitiveness and organizational strength has vanished. This may be indicative of the inefficacy of organization, it may reflect the inability of parties to counteract or copy organizational innovations,[4] or, as we speculated earlier, it may be that the nationalization of the parties, with organization building processes being instigated from the national party committees, has erased the relationship between competitiveness and organizational strength. Thus we are compelled to reject this version of Key's hypothesis: non-competitiveness is not detrimental to party organizational strength.

TABLE 5.2.
Party Organizational Strength and Interparty Competition.

	Interparty Competition Scores 1974–1980			
	One-party Democratic	Modified one-party Democratic	Two-party Competitive	Modified one-party Republican
Average Democratic POS	−.86 (7)	−.33 (15)	−.49 (12)	—[a]
Average Republican POS	.27 (6)	.34 (18)	.43 (20)	—[a]

[a]Too few cases to report.

Relative Electoral Success, Interparty Competition, and Change in Organizational Strength

The foregoing analysis is limited in that it does not control for the original condition of the party organization, that is, instead of average strength, the more appropriate dependent variable for the analysis is change in strength. The hypothesis properly stated is that interparty competition and relative electoral success are related to changes in party organizational strength. This is the second hypothesis to be tested.

The data requirements for testing this hypothesis are more onerous in that two data points are necessary for each party organization. Consequently, the number of cases upon which the analysis is based is somewhat limited and the generalizability and stability of the findings are suspect. As a means of increasing the number of cases, we focus on decade long averages for the party organizational strength measure. Where the data are available, we have scored each party on its average strength in the 1960s and in the 1970s. For the Democrats, we are able to derive scores for 24 parties in the 1960s and 46 parties in the 1970s, with all 24 of the parties from the earlier period being represented in the later period. Comparable figures for the Republicans are 36 parties in the 1960s and 46 in the 1970s, with 33 parties represented in both decades. The relevant data are presented in Table 5.3.

For neither the Republicans nor Democrats is there a relationship between change in the strength of the party organizations and earlier levels of inter-party competition, with no tendency for the electorally stronger parties to have become organizationally stronger. The most competitive parties have changed (on average) the least (.05 for the Democrats, .11 for the

TABLE 5.3.
Correlation of Change in Party Organizational Strength and Interparty Competition.

	Interparty Competition (1946–1963)			
	One-party Democratic	Modified One-party Democratic	Two-party Competitive	Modified One-party Republican
Average POS—1960s[a]				
Democrats	−.66 (4)	−.57 (4)	−.16 (12)	.50 (4)
Republicans	.17 (7)	−.54 (6)	.27 (15)	.51 (8)
Average POS—1970s[b]				
Democrats	−.75 (10)	−.34 (7)	−.32 (19)	−.44 (10)
Republicans	.41 (10)	−.02 (7)	.39 (19)	.46 (10)
Change in POS—1960s to 1970s[c]				
Democrats	.13 (4)	.38 (4)	.05 (12)	−.25 (4)
Republicans	.43 (6)	.40 (5)	.11 (14)	−.19 (8)

[a]The correlation of the linear (folded) measure of competition and organizational strength for the Democrats is .01 (24); for the Republicans it is .09 (36).

[b]The correlation of the linear (folded) measure of competition and organizational strength for the Democrats is −.18 (46); for the Republicans it is .06 (46).

[c]The correlation of the linear (folded) measure of competition and change in organizational strength for the Democrats is −.01 (24); for the Republicans it is .04 (33).

Republicans), but generally competitiveness and success are unrelated to change in organizational strength. Republican organizations have become stronger in those states in which they were electorally less successful, perhaps as a conscious, but not overly successful, attempt to attract votes through organizational effort. The states in which the GOP showed the most marked increases in organizational strength are North Carolina, Washington, Georgia, Arizona, and Maine, while the greatest decreases were observed in Vermont, Michigan and Iowa. The relationship is not particularly strong and therefore should not be overemphasized, however, it appears that electoral weakness, in contrast to noncompetitiveness, has indeed stimulated the Republicans to organizational development. There is even a slight tendency for the electorally dominant organizations to have declined in strength. Thus, for the Republicans, there is some support for the hypothesis that strength is related to prior success even if not to prior competitiveness. For Democrats, strength is related to neither variable.

TABLE 5.4.
Change in Organizational Strength and Change in Relative Electoral Success, 1960–1980

Change in Organizational Strength, 1960s to 1970s	Change in Relative Electoral Success 1963–1973 to 1974–1980 (percent)		
	Republican Increase	No Change	Democratic Increase
Democrats			
Declining Strength	— (0)	33.3 (5)	44.4 (4)
No Change	— (0)	33.3 (5)	22.2 (2)
Increasing Strength	— (0)	33.3 (5)	33.3 (3)
Totals	— (0)	100.0 (15)	100.0 (9)
		Gamma = −.11	
Republicans			
Declining Strength	— (0)	14.3 (3)	16.7 (2)
No Change	— (0)	52.4 (11)	58.3 (7)
Increasing Strength	— (0)	33.3 (7)	25.0 (3)
Totals	— (0)	100.0 (21)	100.0 (12)
		Gamma = −.15	

Change in Relative Electoral Success and Change in Party Organizational Strength

The relationship can also be scrutinized from the perspective of change in relative electoral success and change in party organizational strength (Hypothesis 3). In terms of change from 1963–1973 to 1974–1980, the data in Table 5.4 reveal that the two variables are not strongly related for the Democrats. The parties in states with greater increases in Democratic electoral success seem not to have experienced any greater increases or decreases in organizational strength. However, care must be exercised in interpreting this relationship. Although the POS scores of nine parties declined, none of the 24 parties experienced a significant decline in RES; most of the change was indeed miniscule. Of the nine state parties experiencing significantly greater RES, four declined in POS, while three increased. Whatever causes the party's electoral fortunes to vary does not cause the strength of party organizations to vary as well.

Among the 33 Republican state parties for which data are available the correlation between changing success and changing strength is insignificant. In no states did the Republicans increase in electoral strength, so this portion of the hypothesis cannot be tested. However, there is virtually no difference between those organizations that experience a decline in their party's RES and those that did not. An illustration or two can elucidate this point. The Vermont Republican organization declined the most dramatically, while the North Carolina Republicans registered the greatest increase in POS. But in Vermont the RES index moved in the Democratic direction by .03, slightly less than average, and in North Carolina it changed by .08, slightly more than average. Inspection of the scattergram further confirms that no relationship exists.

Perhaps the most extreme illustrations of this point are the Ohio and Virginia Democratic parties. In Ohio, the following changes have occurred in the past two decades:

	$t-3$	$t-2$	$t-1$	t
Democratic POS	—	.277	1.811	−1.191
Republican POS	—	—	1.206	1.186

Change in Relative Electoral Success		
$t-2$ to $t-1$	$t-1$ to t	$t-2$ to t
+.017	+.222	+.239

(Note that POS ranges from approximately −3.0 to +3.0.) Thus, it can be seen that the strength of the Democratic party organization oscillated, while the Republican organization changed little, although both changes occurred within the context of an increase in Democratic RES in the 1970s. Similarly, in Virginia the electoral success of the Democrats has declined, but in the face of increasing Democratic organizational strength and little change in Republican POS. Other examples would confirm that for both the Democrats and Republicans, POS does not generally covary with RES.

Summary

Are party organizational strength and interparty competition related? Operating within a framework in which POS is a central concern, it would be attractive to state the expectation that POS will determine levels of IPC/RES. We have reviewed some of the difficulties of measuring such a relationship and acknowledged the record of the Democratic party in the

South which caused V. O. Key to formulate the alternative expectation that IPC determines POS. Testing for either relationship would require longitudinal analysis beyond that which our data permits. But cross-sectional testing of the IPC-POS relationship in four time periods shows strong relationships in the earliest and no relationship in the most recent period. In the early 1960s, while both parties exhibited a strong relationship between RES and POS, for the Democrats, organizational weakness was associated with high levels of RES, while for the Republicans, strength was so associated. That relationship was eroded by the late 1970s, when no significant association could be demonstrated between POS and RES for either party. Attacking the change question more directly by constructing a change variable for POS and investigating the relationship between IPC and change in POS, we again find party differences, although within the context of weak relationships. We may have circumstantial evidence of the movement of both parties toward a parity of organizational efficacy in electoral politics.

It may be more reasonable to consider the effect of POS on outcomes in races for specific offices. In the next section of this chapter, we turn to the relationship between POS and gubernatorial electoral success.

PARTY ORGANIZATIONAL STRENGTH AND GUBERNATORIAL ELECTIONS: A DYNAMIC ANALYSIS

The most likely discernable impact of state party organizational strength is on the outcomes of gubernatorial elections. American parties are "executive centered coalitions" (James, 1974, p. 247 ff), and traditionally party organizations have been the creatures of governors, so to the extent that the organization has resources it is likely that governors and gubernatorial candidates will profit from them. As the most significant political office in the state, it is unlikely that party organizations will be uninvolved in the contests for governor. Moreover, the gubernatorial office is strategically related to office opportunity structures within the party organization. Governors may designate, veto, or play a more subtle role in the selection of the state party chair. Indeed, the governor may come from a background of party office-holding, or move on to a party position after leaving public office.

The state party organizations serve "the self-interests of their members" by pressing for a relationship of influence with "the most potent political power in [the] state" (Muchmore and Beyle, 1980, pp. 121–22). A governor beholden to the party for effective electoral support can be a source of help in fundraising, generating benefits such as patronage, and can help with candidate recruitment. And, the gubernatorial office provides a useful focal point for the campaign. The benefits are not one-sided either since the governor has incentives to cooperate with and strengthen the state party organization. Interviews with outgoing governors (National Governors' Association, 1981; Muchmore and Beyle, 1980, pp. 123–24) suggest that, while qualified in their recognition of the policy and patronage role of parties, the governors are fully cognizant that the party can be of importance in the renomination process, and that the governors look to the state party as a source of effective help with their legislative programs. A handbook for new governors, issued by the National Governors' Association in 1978, cautioned the chief executives who had been elected in campaigns conducted relatively independently of the party "that this individualistic approach is counterproductive in the conduct of the office itself" (cited in Jewell and Olson, 1982, p. 168).

In summary, strong parties have more to gain or lose in gubernatorial elections than in other elections, and hence a large incentive to influence their outcomes. Governors have much to gain from responsive state party organizations, and it is a reasonably familiar argument that "the more successful the governor is as party leader, the more successful he is as head of state" (Morehouse, 1976, p. 196). Hence it might be expected that a candidate with the foresight to anticipate the party needs of the governor, or an incumbent governor running for re-election, would be receptive to some party role in the campaign. Similarly, state parties will be under heavy incentive to demonstrate their usefulness to the next governor, and to do so by laying some claim to responsibility for a successful campaign.

A Model of Organizational Strength and Gubernatorial Electoral Success

We posit that gubernatorial electoral success is a function of (1) the relative strength of the state party organizations; (2) the relative emphasis the organization places on relations with the governor (gubernatorial linkage); (3) the relative strength of the local party organizations; (4) the degree to which local party organizations are integrated with their state party organizations; (5) the strength of extra-party organizations within the state; and (6) historical and demographic attributes of the state, attributes best summarized by the concept of the "normal vote." Because it is the major control variable, we begin with a discussion of this last factor, which permits us to measure success in terms of increments from the "normal vote."

Incremental Electoral Success

There are several major requisites for measuring electoral success so that the impact of party organizational strength on it can be determined. First, in order that the peculiarities of particular elections should not have an overriding effect on the analysis, we have averaged electoral outcomes over a period of years. Since in the analysis that follows we employ a party organizational strength measure for the last half of the decade of the 1970s, we have also calculated the mean success scores for the period 1975–1980. The impact of idiosyncratic perturbations is thus minimized to some degree as is the effect of national trends. Second, electoral success must not be treated as an absolute concept. Success is relative to the history or tradition of the party's prior success. These differences can be summarized by the concept of the normal vote. The parties differ in competitiveness in the different states, and it is not useful to penalize the hypothesis that organizational strength has an effect by ignoring these differences. Success must be measured in terms of change or deviation from the normal vote, that is as an increment or decrement above or below what would be expected on the basis of historical patterns of electoral competitiveness.

These considerations have guided the construction of the electoral success measures. Specifically, the measure of success in gubernatorial elections in the period 1975–1980 was constructed as follows:

1. The percentage of the two-party vote that was cast for the Democratic candidate was calculated for each election in the period.
2. These percentages were averaged across all elections between 1975 and 1980.
3. The average percentages were then regressed on averages for the periods 1970–1974 and 1965–1969. The averages for the two earlier periods were constructed in the same way as those for the late 1970s, and are taken as surrogates for the normal vote in the state. In using two distinct variables to represent prior success, we allow the effect of immediate past history (i.e., the preceding half decade) to be statistically different than the effect of more intermediate past history (i.e., the period from 10 to 5 years in the past).
4. Residuals were then calculated, indicating the degree to which the pattern of success in the period 1975–1980 is an increment or a decrement above or below that to be expected on the basis of the electoral competitiveness of the party in the state in the last decade.[5] In this sense, electoral success is measured in terms of incremental change from the normal vote.

Relative State Party Organizational Strength

In the analysis that follows, party organizational strength is measured in terms of the relative strength of the Democratic state party organization. The specific measure employed is the ratio of Democratic strength to the total organizational strength of the two parties (i.e., Democratic plus Republican strength). This measure is particularly useful for the analysis of electoral success in that it recognizes that the organizational strength of one party may be counteracted by the strength of the other party. This measure also controls for environmental and historical factors that may depress or enhance the strength of both parties. While a state may be deficient in organizational resources, it is one party's advantage in strength over the other, not the overall weakness of both, that is relevant for the analysis. Thus, on this measure, it is possible for the Democrats in a state with weak party organizations to achieve a relative strength score identical to that of a Democratic party in a state with strong party organizations. The isomorphism of the strength and success measures is of advantage both from the statistical and theoretical pespectives.

We are able to score 32 of the 39 non-southern states on this ratio of organizational strength. The mean score is 44.3 (standard deviation = 7.6), indicating that in the average state the Democrats control about 44 percent of the total two-party organizational strength in the state. In only eight states (Michigan, North Dakota, Rhode Island, Utah, Pennsylvania, Idaho, Massachusetts, and Kentucky) do the Democrats control more than 50 percent of the organizational resources, and the maximum percentage is still a fairly low 58 percent. In contrast, in Vermont the Republican party organization commands nearly 75 percent of that state's party organizational resources. Other states in which there is a substantial Republican advantage include: Ohio, Illinois, Indiana, New York, Nevada, Iowa, and Minnesota. Despite what might appear to be significant regional differences, there is very little difference across the three regions in relative organizational strength.

Local Party Organizational Strength

At the local level, a very similar conceptual approach to organizational strength was adopted. Using somewhat different indicators, to reflect the differences in level of bureaucratization and programmatic activities of state and local party organizations (see Chapter 3), a summary measure of organizational strength was constructed through factor analysis. Because electoral success is measured as a state-level attribute (the unit of analysis is the state), it is necessary to conceptualize aggregate local party strength as an attribute of states, that can affect electoral outcomes at the state level. We run some risk in the aggregated analysis of committing the ecological fallacy, but there are few alternatives to this form of cross-level analysis.

In 1069 of the counties responding to our mail questionnaires, responses were received from both the Democratic and Republican party organizations, thus allowing the calculation of aggregated relative strength scores. Considering the absolute POS scores, as distinguished from relative strength scores, the mean Republican local party POS score for 32 non-southern states is .30, while the Democratic average is .15. Among the Democrats, the county-equivalent party organizations in the Northeast are the strongest, with the organization in the Midwest and West about equal in strength (and southern organizations substantially weaker). The Republican pattern is similar to the Democratic.

In a fashion analogous to that employed at the level of state party organizations, a ratio indicating the relative strength of the local Democratic parties can be constructed. This ratio must, of course, be calculated prior to aggregation. The average percentage of local party strength controlled by the Democrats is 49.1 across 31 non-southern states, indicating fairly balanced organizational strength.[6] Only slight regional variation can be found (even in the South the average ratio is 51.3). Interestingly, the correlation between relative state organizational strength and relative local organizational strength (aggregated) is practically zero.

Integration of State and Local Party Organizations

A concern for parties as organizations leads to consideration of the relationships among party units, or party integration. In Chapter 4, party integration is defined as interdependence of different strata of party organizations. Interdependence between the state and local parties implies joint activity toward common goals, or at least party organizations at different levels assisting one another in achieving their goals. When one level of organization consistently exploits another for its own purposes, the reciprocity necessary to interdependence is absent and integration is marginal. Thus, party integration implies commonality and reciprocity.

"Degree of integration" is taken to be an attribute of each local party organization. Consequently, a measure of integration for each local party has been constructed from the questionnaire responses of the local party leaders. Six sub-dimensions of party integration are identified: (1) the legal relationship of state and local parties; (2) the degree of structural integration of state and local parties; (3) the level of communication between organizations; (4) state party support for local party activity; (5) joint state-local programs; and (6) state party involvement in the selection of local leaders. The indicators are moderately intercorrelated, and consequently reveal a unidimensional structure when factor analyzed. These items can be used to calculate a measure of party integration. The range of the index is from 0 to 60; its mean is 20.4, and its standard deviation is 12.2. Less than 10 percent of the parties score 40 or above on the measure, but only 3 percent have a score of 0. Little party-related variability in the index is apparent, with Republican county organizations scoring significantly (statistically) but only slightly higher than Democratic organizations. There is a moderate tendency for stronger local parties to be better integrated with their state organizations ($r = .37$).

Party-Government Linkage

In Chapter 6, "linkage" will be conceptually defined as requiring (1) a high level of interaction between officeholders and the party organization, and (2) a reciprocal relationship between the officeholders and the party organization.

Gubernatorial linkage. A summary index of state party-gubernatorial linkage was derived from separate indices constructed for organizational involvement in party affairs, and for gubernatorial involvement in party affairs. The median score on the resulting index (ranging from 0 to 6) is 3.9, suggesting that state party organizations are at least moderately linked with their governors. Indeed, over one-third of the party organizations have a fairly high level of linkage (i.e., score of 5 or 6). High linkage levels usually result from a congruence of interests, a mutual interdependence, and a mutual willingness to accommodate, although the general pattern of linkage is one of the governor responding to actions initiated by the state party organizations, rather than actively directing the organization. There is a slight, but statistically insignificant, tendency for Republican state party organizations to be more highly linked with their governors than are the Democrats. Because the primary indicators of party-government relations were only asked during the interviews with the state party leaders in the sample states, only 30 state parties can be scored on gubernatorial linkages (half of the 54 sample state parties augmented by a few out-parties whose chairs had worked with the predecessor governor).

Legislative linkage. While the emphasis on interdependence and reciprocity applies to both gubernatorial and legislative linkage, gubernatorial and legislative offices and constituencies are quite different and consequently the measures are somewhat different. Linkage with the state legislative leadership is measured by levels of interaction within three substantive areas: (1) internal party affairs; (2) electoral and constituency affairs; and (3) policy matters. While there are some interesting differences in how Republican and Democratic state party organizations relate to their legislators, overall, the scores of the Democratic and Republican organizations on the summary measure of linkage with the state legislative parties are not greatly or statistically dissimilar.

Extra-party Organizations

There is an obvious need to control the strength of extra-party organizations in considering the determinants of electoral success. The need is intensified by the fact that the effect is interactive with party; the influence of extra-party organizations on electoral outcomes no doubt interacts with party. For instance, it is easy to imagine that labor organizations provide substantial financial support and voter mobilization activity to Democratic candidates, thus obviating the need for the party organization to provide such support. To the extent that the extra-party organizations and parties are aligned in their efforts in elections, correlations of strength and success will over-estimate the impact of the party organization. If extra-party organizations and parties are in opposition, the impact of the party organization will be underestimated.

We assume that extra-party organizations have some independent impact on electoral success. That is, we assume that extra-party organizations are effective in utilizing their resources to influence electoral outcomes. (Note that the dependent variable in our analysis is not the outcome in a particular election but rather the trend in outcomes, as represented by the average vote over a five-year period, residualized for the normal vote, thus the dependent variable is the average increment.)

We expect that extra-party organizations may differentially affect the two parties. If the two parties rely to differing degrees on extra-party organizations for support, then the correlations of strength and success will not accurately portray the impact of organization on electoral outcomes. In this analysis we use the percentage of the labor force that is unionized as a surrogate for the strength of extra-party organizations within the state. Because of their greater ability to derive support from extra-party organizations, the strength of the Democratic state parties will appear to have a lesser impact on electoral success than does the strength of the Republicans.

Analytical Framework

The basic hypothesis we address is that incremental electoral success is in part a function of the strength of the party organizations within the states, all other things being equal. Although the basic hypothesis is relatively simple, many factors that complicate the model must be considered, including:

1. Regional effects. Because of the peculiar history of party competition in the South, we have, as indicated, excluded that region from all of the analysis.
2. Party effects. It has been earlier established that the Democratic and Republican state party organizations differ dramatically in strength (although the local parties do not). Moreover, our analyses have consistently demonstrated marked party differences in the causes and consequences of organizational strength. Thus, this analysis of strength and success will be segregated by party.
3. Curvilinear effects. It should not be expected that the relationship between strength and success is linear. There is no doubt a threshold (around 60 percent of the vote) beyond which increments in strength have little impact on success. A similar limit at very low levels of success probably also exists. This effect is mitigated somewhat, but not completely, by the useage of incremental success as the dependent variable. Thus, the analysis must be sensitive to the possibility of a cubic relationship.

Analysis

We test five hypotheses on the relationship of attributes of party organization to party gubernatorial electoral success:

H4: The party advantaged in state level organizational strength will experience higher levels of gubernatorial electoral success than the organizationally disadvantaged party.

H5: The party advantaged in local level organizational strength will experience higher levels of gubernatorial electoral success than the organizationally disadvantaged party.

H6: Levels of party integration are associated with levels of party gubernatorial electoral success.

H7: Levels of party-governor linkage are associated with levels of party gubernatorial electoral success.

H8: Levels of party-legislative linkage are associated with levels of party gubernatorial electoral success.

The analysis of the impact of the attributes of party organization on electoral success is summarized in Table 5.5, and the effect of controlling for extra-party organizations is reported in the text that follows.

The first hypothesis to be tested (H4) is simply that where Democratic state party organizations have the advantage in terms of organizational strength over the Republican party organization, the Democratic candidate

TABLE 5.5.
The Impact of Organizational Attributes on Gubernatorial Electoral Success, 1975–1980.

	Bivariate Correlations Non-South
State Party Organizational Strength	
Average—Democrats	.23 (35)
Average—Republicans	−.33 (35)
Ratio—Democrats/Republicans	.46 (32)
Local Party Organizational Strength	
Average—Democrats	.02 (32)
Average—Republicans	.04 (32)
Ratio—Democrats/Republicans	−.00 (31)
State-Local Party Integration	
Average—Democrats	.22 (32)
Average—Republicans	.01 (31)
Local Strength Weighted by Integration	
Average—Democrats	.11 (32)
Average—Republicans	.18 (31)
Ratio—Democrats/Republicans	.15 (29)
State Party Linkage with Officeholders	
Gubernatorial—Democrats	.01 (13)
Gubernatorial—Republicans	.27 (10)
Legislative—Democrats	−.46 (19)
Legislative—Republicans	−.16 (20)

for governor will tend to be more successful.[7] This hypothesis receives substantial support: the correlation between relative Democratic strength and incremental Democratic success is +.46 for 32 non-southern states in the last half of the 1970s. This relationship is substantially stronger than that between absolute Democratic strength and success ($r = .23$) and absolute Republican strength and success ($r = .33$), a finding compatible with the argument that the electoral impact of the strength of the state party organization can be neutralized by the strength of the opposite party organization. There is some evidence that where the Democrats are organizationally superior, the payoff in terms of electoral outcomes of increments of strength is somewhat greater than it is for Republican organizations that are superior, although the number of instances of Democratic dominance is too small ($n = 8$) for this result to be very stable. In general, we conclude that state-level organizational strength makes a difference in gubernatorial races.

We find no similar effect of local party organizational strength on gubernatorial elections (H5). In terms of neither absolute nor relative local strength is there any relationship with gubernatorial success, although the aggregated nature of the indicator must be taken into consideration. If local strength makes little difference, it is not surprising to observe that levels of state-local integration do not affect electoral success (H6). Even when we weight the strength of each local party organization (i.e., prior to aggregation) by the degree to which it is integrated with the state party, as a means of indicating the degree to which local strength is available to the state party to be mobilized for the purposes of electing the governor, only very slight relationships are observed. The strength of local party organizations simply does not seem to matter much in gubernatorial elections.[8]

There is only a slight tendency, and only for the Republicans, for levels of party-governor linkage to relate to gubernatorial electoral success (H7). (Note that the numbers of cases upon which these correlations are based are quite small: 10 for the Republicans and 13 for the Democrats.) The results for the relationships of legislative linkage to success are a bit different (H8). For Republicans, the relationship is inconsequential ($r = -.16$; $N = 20$). For Democrats, however, the relationship is moderate ($r = -.46$; $N = 19$). For Democrats, there seems to be considerable tension between gubernatorial and legislative linkage, with strong legislative linkages associated with weak gubernatorial linkages. In Chapter 6 we will suggest that some Democratic state party organizations may retreat to the state legislature in part as a means of counteracting a governor antagonistic to the party. Here we see further support for that proposition. Where linkage with the legislature is strong, Democratic gubernatorial electoral success is weak, possibly because the state party organization is withholding its resources from the governor. This is further evidence that party organizations make a difference (at least for the Democrats); where their resources are denied candidates, Democratic gubernatorial candidates seem to suffer.

A more sophisticated test of this hypothesis requires that the following equation be estimated:

$$\gamma = bX_1 + bX_2 + b(X_1 X_2),$$

where

$$\gamma = \text{gubernatorial electoral success,}$$
$$X_1 = \text{state party organizational strength,}$$
$$X_2 = \text{state party-gubernatorial linkage, and}$$
$$X_1 X_2 = \text{the interaction of strength and linkage.}$$

The equation posits that linkage serves as a weight to be attached to strength, or it might be thought of as a switch. Where linkage exists, the switch is open and the strength of the party organization can flow to the governor. Where linkage does not exist, the switch is closed, and the governor is denied party resources. Though we cannot test this hypothesis because of the small number of cases available to us, and though we believe that the hypothesis would only be supported for the Democrats, this is a likely addition to a comprehensive theory of the effect of party organizations on electoral outcomes.

To control for extra-party organizations, analysis was undertaken using the percentage of the labor force that is unionized as a surrogate for the strength of extra-party organizations within the state. A simple test of the influence of this variable on relative gubernatorial success was conducted. The union membership variable was entered into a regression equation after state and local party organizational strength scores were entered.

For neither the Republicans nor the Democrats did the addition of this variable contribute significantly to the explanation of gubernatorial electoral success, and unionization had no direct (i.e., bivariate) relationship to gubernatorial success.

Gubernatorial outcomes are divorced from the normal vote. Gubernatorial success at time t is virtually unrelated to success at $t-1$. This may be due to declining levels of party identification, but it may also be associated with increasing effects of the state party organizations. While it is the general practice to attribute such results to the erosion of parties and the rise of new forms of organizational influence in electoral politics, it may with equal justification be surmised that the reason why there is so little continuity in gubernatorial vote patterns is because of a new, significant actor in the electoral arena: the party organization. Note also that while this analysis excludes the South, Republican inroads at the state office level in the South have been uneven and limited to the gubernatorial level. We suspect such inroads are largely a function of the role of Republican state party organizations.

Does Party Make a Difference?

We have explored permutations of V. O. Key's thesis that relative electoral success and interparty competition are related to the strengthening of party organizations. The inverse relationship found for Democratic parties, and the expected relationship found for the electorally subordinate Republican parties in the early 1960s, were followed by a succession of five-year eras in which interparty competition appeared to have no impact upon organizational strength for either party. If the party organizations were in the low state generally assumed in the 1950s, the early 1960s may have been a developmental period for state party organizations. It was the "reconstruction of party organization" which Key stressed as an expected consequence of increasing competition, and it may well be that for a brief but critical period his expected relationship obtained. Beyond a threshold level of organizational strength, and with both competition and strength rising, the equilibrating adjustments between the two may, as we have suggested, have obscured or effaced the relationship.

Looking at the relationship between party strength and electoral success in gubernatorial races, we again find evidence of the electoral relevance of party organization. The organizationally stronger of the two state parties (the party which has the disproportionate share of the state's party organizational resources) will tend to achieve the higher increments of gubernatorial votes. If we can impute an electoral motive to the quest for party organizational strength, it must be to enhance the party's electoral performance, and this relationship is clearly evidenced in the analysis presented.

NOTES

1. There are a host of nuances to the Ranney measure, two of which have considerable importance for our work. First, it is based exclusively on state-level elections, ignoring completely federal legislative and presidential elections. Less obvious is the fact that the measure is relatively more sensitive to state legislative success than to gubernatorial success. Using data for the period 1974 to 1980 (see Bibby, et al., 1983), the correlations between the overall index and the average percentage of Democratic vote of the upper and lower chambers of the state legislatures are both .96, while the correlation of the index with the average percentage of the popular vote cast for the Democratic candidate for governor is only .61. This must be borne in mind in the analysis that follows.

2. Ranney sought a relationship between his measure and "centralized authority" of state party organizations, and found it to be "slight at best, and both Republicans and Democrats are highly decentralized in many of our most competitive two-party states" (1965, p. 71). However, lack of appropriate measures for the party organizations prevented Ranney from conducting a formal test of the hypothesis.

3. Note, for example, the 1982 Hunt Commission's acknowledgment of "the remarkable financial and organizational successes of the national Republican Party" as partial indication of party renewal. The report goes on to cite "some comparable signs of vitality and progress in our own party." (The Commission on Presidential Nomination, *Final Report to the Democratic National Committee*, March 31, 1982, p. 1., Washington, D.C., Democratic National Committee, 1982.) The early 1980s saw publication of numerous newspaper stories on the condition of the parties, and featuring quotations in which the DNC or Democratic congressional campaign committee staff cite Republican organizational accomplishments as setting standards to be matched.

4. Though we cannot sort out the causal processes, there is (as we have observed in Chapter 4) a fairly substantial tendency for the strength of the Democratic and

Republican organizations in the states to covary. The correlation using strength scores from the 1960s was .78 ($N = 20$); for the 1970s, the correlation was .32 ($N = 43$). Using indicators of changing strength from the 1960s to the 1970s, the correlation was .30 (18). Several interpretations of these data are possible. In the 1960s, it is possible that the parties either copied innovations from one another, or that they responded similarly to the environmental stimuli of their states. In the 1970s there is still some of this tendency; however, it is much weakened. One obvious possibility is that non-indigenous, party-specific factors have contributed to the development of strong party organizations. The most obvious factor is the party's national committeee. There might be a tendency to believe that this is largely a result of activity on the part of the Republican National Committee, but perhaps that is not so. If external intervention is the primary determinant of party organizational strength, and if the RNC were especially effective at building party organizations, then we should expect to see lower correlations between the strength scores of the 1960s and those of the 1970s for the Republicans as compared to the Democrats. The correlation for the 33 Republican parties for which we have scores from both decades is .51, for the 24 Democratic parties, the correlation is .64. Thus, there is only marginally greater continuity for the Democrats than for the Republicans. We have noted earlier (see chapter 4, and Huckshorn, et al., 1982b) that the DNC, even absent the organizational resources of the RNC, seems to have been able to play a significant role in spurring the state parties to organizational development. Generally, the processes might not differ a great deal between the two parties.

5. There is substantial and surprising variability in the results of the regression for gubernatorial races as compared to similar measures for state legislative, federal legislative, and presidential races during the same period. Excluding the South, the amounts of variance explained by the regressions are: state legislative, 88.3 percent; presidential, 64.3 percent; congressional, 31.1 percent; and gubernatorial, 4.3 percent. There are, no doubt, many explanations for these findings, probably reflecting the varying strength of party attachments at the state and federal levels; the relative salience of different levels of politics; the amount of campaign spending and consequently the availability of information that might override a vote decision based on party identification; and incumbency effects (e.g., the relative infrequency of gubernatorial incumbents). To sort out a theoretical explanation for the findings is, however, beyond the scope of this research.

Donald A. Gross (1981) analyzes two-party competition over two decades, and makes a number of findings relevant to electoral success analysis:

Since 1952, "presidential competition has been quite divorced from competition in non-presidential elections. Conversely, since 1952 the means of non-presidential elections tend to go up and down together in a relatively consistent pattern" (p. 17). "For the most part, with only a few exceptions like the presidential election of 1968, the mean levels of competition in all types of elections in non-southern states has remained about the same since 1932" (p. 21). In the South, one partyism is eliminated at the presidential level first. This process commenced in 1948 and 12 to 16 years later we begin to see significant increases in the mean level of competition in other types of elections. It is the mean level of competition in gubernatorial races that first approximates the levels associated with presidential elections, followed by the U.S. Senate, with House races lagging significantly behind the other races (p. 22).

6. We were unwilling to include states for which we had responses from both parties for fewer than five counties. This standard automatically excludes some states (e.g., Delaware, that have fewer than five counties), however, the alternative procedure of stipulating a minimum standard in terms of the ratio of counties in the state for which responses from both parties are available presents even more problems. An alternative approach is to score the states on the basis of responses from all of the counties irrespective of whether we have a response from the opposition party in the county. Such a strategy allows much more stable estimates of aggregate local party strength but precludes the construction of variables indicating the relative strength of the local parties in the counties. Depending upon the usage, a certain possibility of commiting the ecological fallacy exists, nonetheless, the two strategies produce quite similar results. At the state level ($N = 32$ non-southern states), the correlation for the Democrats is .95; for the Republicans it is .97.

7. The reader is reminded that electoral success is defined in terms of deviation from the normal vote. Thus, when we speak of success we refer to the increment in the electoral outcome over and above what would have been expected on the basis of historical voting patterns and demographic attributes of the state.

8. We cannot determine whether this finding is an artifact of the aggregation process.

6

Party Relationships with Elected Officeholders: Linkage

"Linkage" has become a well defined subfield since V. O. Key (1961, p. 410) introduced the term to designate the interrelationships between the public, various intermediating structures such as political parties, and public officeholders. For Key, "linkage" designated the "interplay [that] occurs between mass opinion and government," and conditions the actions of government (p. 423).[1] Linkage processes were seen by Key to involve intermediating agencies. Since linkage relationships involve "interplay" or interaction, government not only is hypothesized to be conditioned by opinion, but it also "attempts to mold public opinion toward support of the programs and policies it espouses" (p. 422). Intermediating agencies between public and government are not mere conduits of opinion, but are influenced by and seek to influence it. Although political parties are prime examples of linkage mechanisms, Key believed American parties to be poorly equipped to perform that role (p. 452).

Perhaps because of difficulties in securing systematic data, there have been few studies of American party units as linkage mechanisms (Marvick, 1980). Moreover, some of the literature exhibits a pronounced tendency to equate linkage with representation (a point stressed by Lawson, 1980, p. 8, and Wahlke, 1971). That is to say, studies of "linkage" frequently skip over intermediating processes in their effort to establish a connection between public opinion, the behaviors of elected officeholders, and public policy.

The units of linkage that we study are the state party central committees and the parties' governors and state legislators. Our central concern is whether the strength of party organizations appears to influence their relationships with party officeholders, not whether there is a relationship between opinion and policy.[2] Thus we operate at one end of the public-government linkage model, working with party and government rather than party and public. We are not concerned with party as agent of government in linkage processes directed toward the public.

Furthermore, we conceptualize linkage to include an element of reciprocity. The measures developed to permit us to test for the hypothesized relationship between party organizational strength and linkage are so weighted as to impose a harsh penalty for the absence of reciprocity in the relationships. Hence, if we were to imagine applying the measure to a vestigial party machine that manipulates the behaviors of officeholders, or to a governor who has transformed the party into a personal machine, these would exemplify low linkage relationships in consequence of their low interactive quotients. When viewed in this way, linkage requires two participants having overlapping (but not identical or enclaved) constituencies with some independence in resource bases, and hence, relationships that lean strongly toward interdependence.

PARTY-GOVERNMENT LINKAGE

Party and Governor

Although convention assigns the titular role of party leader to the American president and to the governor (at least in many states), the effective melding of these two roles is infrequent. For this and other reasons, it might be expected that we would not expect strong patterns of linkage between state party organizations and governors. On the other hand, there might well be some factors operative at the state and even national levels in the United States that work contrary to those expectations. In a generally decentralized governmental system, in which chief department officers and even the civil service can be largely autonomous of gubernatorial control, a strong party organization might be in a position to perform significant services for the chief executive. It may also be that governors who are strong and effective tend to be assertive of a party leadership role. The party's role in electoral politics and processes should also not be discounted.

Though analytically distinct, the relations of the state party to the governor and the legislators are functionally intertwined. Separation of powers means that the legislators are elected independently of the governor and must first respond to constituency demands (to the extent that they exist) if they are to survive. The decentralized nature of American politics, plus the widespread use of the direct primary to nominate legislative candidates, means that governors do not control the recruitment and nomination of those who will carry their party's banner in the general election. Interviews conducted with outgoing governors (National Governors' Association, 1981;

Muchmore and Beyle, 1980, pp. 123–24) suggest that, while qualified in their recognition of the policy and patronage role of parties, governors look to the state party for help with their legislative program. Further, there is considerable cognizance among the governors of the party's role in the renomination process.

Moreover, the state chairmanship and the governorship may be linked by office ambition. For some governors, the party position has been a waystop enroute to the executive mansion. In the period 1962 to 1980, 12 former state party chairs were elected governor (4 Republicans and 8 Democrats). Another 20 (13 Republicans and 7 Democrats) sought the office, but lost in either the primary or the general election (Huckshorn, et al., 1982a, p. 31; and Beyle, 1983, Figure 6.1, p. 184).

When the state and local parties are organizationally strong and integrated, the state party should be in a better position to serve "the self-interest of their members" by pressing for a relationship of influence with "the most potent political power in [the] state" (Muchmore and Beyle, 1980, pp. 121–22). Reciprocally, the governor has heavier incentive to placate the party and make it an adjunct to the renominating and election campaign when the party at the state level is not only well organized, but in a favorable position to mobilize the resources of the county parties. Hence we would expect that state parties that are both organizationally strong and integrated will exhibit higher levels of integration with the governor than parties that are strong but not integrated.

Measuring Linkage with the Governor

In order to determine levels of party-governor linkage, conceptualized as requiring reciprocity, it is necessary to construct measures of the degree of the party organization's involvement in gubernatorial affairs and the degree of gubernatorial involvement in party affairs. Indicators of each of these dimensions have been constructed from the responses of the state chairs and executive directors to items from the interview protocol. Except for campaign assistance, all data reported here refer to party relations with incumbent governors, not to gubernatorial candidates. The number of governors in our sample is 30 (17 Democrats and 13 Republicans).[3]

Party Organization Involvement in Gubernatorial Affairs

Party organizations can assist governors in three areas: (1) campaigning, (2) patronage, and (3) serving as a spokesperson for them. One-fifth of the state party organizations provide little or no campaign support to gubernatorial candidates, but party differences are substantial. All of the Republican organizations provide such support, but only slightly more than one-half of the Democratic organizations do. Generally, Republican state parties provide more services to their gubernatorial candidates than do supporting Democratic organizations. But there is some tendency for gubernatorial candidates to benefit more from services such as polling and voter mobilization, that benefit the entire party ticket, than from services such as media assistance which are tailored to the needs of specific candidates. The median amount of money contributed to gubernatorial candidates by state party organizations, as reported in 1979–1980, was $39,000 (omitting those parties making no contributions). While Republicans provided equal levels of support to incumbents and non-incumbents, Democratic organizations showed a slight tendency to favor incumbents. Generally, Republican organizations provide more campaign support, more services and more money to a larger proportion of candidates, than do the Democrats. This is probably because they are organizationally stronger and have more resources at their disposal.

State party organizations are also involved in patronage distribution, with 70 percent reporting some level of involvement in state patronage. Some of the chairs described a fairly institutionalized form of party involvement in patronage at the state level (e.g., the vice chair of one state party serves as the governor's patronage secretary), but the most common role is to suggest or to recommend names to the governor. Republican organizations are somewhat more involved in this than Democratic organizations.

The state chairs were also asked whether being "a spokesman for the governor or another elected party leader" was an important aspect of the job. Here there is evidence that the state party organizations are not so well integrated with governors. Over two-thirds of the chairs reported that being a spokesperson for the governor was not important. Party differences on this item are significant, with Democrats attaching much greater importance to the spokesperson role.

Gubernatorial Involvement in State Party Affairs

Three aspects of gubernatorial involvement in party affairs were the subject of probing in the state party leader interviews: (1) the role of the governor in selecting the party chair, (2) the extent to which the state chair sensed the need of gubernatorial approval or clearance before taking some kinds of action, and (3) the general quality of the governor's relationship to the party, including such considerations as the location of initiatives for gubernatorial party activity (does the governor take initiatives, does the governor respond to party initiatives, etc.) and areas of gubernatorial assistance.

Perhaps the most obvious avenue of gubernatorial influence over the party is involvement in the process of selecting the party chair. Most governors are involved in the selection process in some fashion, although substantial party differences exist. Slightly more than one-half of the Democratic state chairs ascribed a determinative role to the governor, ranging from dissuading unwanted candidates for the position to actually designating the chair. The comparable figure for the Republican chairs is only 31 percent. A majority of the Republican chairs reported little or no gubernatorial role in their selection. It may be that the more formal style of interaction between Republican governors and party leaders, reflecting the more bureaucratized Republican state party organizations, accounts for the party differences. This encourages speculation that party-governor integration may be qualitatively different for Democrats and Republicans.

Despite the more significant role of Democratic governors in the selection process, Democratic chairs reported somewhat greater autonomy from the governor in running the state party organization. Nearly two-thirds of the Republican chairs found it necessary to have the governor's support before making major party decisions, but only one-half of the Democrats were so constrained.

The state chairs were also asked to generally characterize the relationship of the governor to the state party organization. Not surprisingly, only a few of the chairs reported the governor had no relationship with the organization. The Democratic chairs overwhelmingly reported the governor only related to the party in an advisory capacity. This is true of nearly one-half of the Republican organizations as well. However, 39 percent of the Republicans, but none of the Democrats, reported their governors were quite responsive to party initiatives. One such initiative is party fundraising and here 39 percent of the Republicans asserted that their governors are active fundraisers for the party. This contrasts to 12 percent of the Democrats claiming such a high level of gubernatorial assistance. Republican governors are also significantly more active in assisting the party in candidate recruitment than are the Democratic governors. Possibly because of the greater amount of fundraising and recruitment activity on the part of Republican organizations, GOP governors have a somewhat higher level of involvement in the party organizations' affairs than do Democratic governors.

TABLE 6.1.

Interactions of Governors and State Party Organizations by Percentages of Parties (27 sample states, 1979–1980).

Interaction	Democrats	Republicans	Total
Organizational Involvement in Gubernatorial Affairs			
Importance of being spokesman for the governor			
not important	58.8	69.2	63.3
important	11.8	30.8	20.0
very important	29.4	0.0	16.7
Party involvement in state patronage			
no role	35.3	23.1	30.0
some role	64.7	76.9	70.0
Campaign services to governor			
none	41.2	0.0	23.3
some	58.8	100.0	76.7
Financial contributions to gubernatorial campaigns			
little or none	50.0	53.8	51.7
$5,000–49,999	37.5	23.1	31.0
greater than $50,000	12.5	23.1	17.2
Gubernatorial Involvement in Organizational Affairs			
Selection of state chair			
little or no role	17.6	53.8	33.3
acquiescence	29.4	15.4	23.3
instrumental role	52.9	30.8	43.3
Necessary to have governor's support before acting			
generally not	52.9	38.5	46.7
on some issues	47.1	61.5	53.3
General characterization of governor's relationship to party			
none	5.9	15.4	10.0
advisory	94.1	46.2	73.3
responsive	0.0	38.5	16.7
Gubernatorial role in candidate recruitment			
little or none	47.1	0.0	26.7
advisory	35.3	84.6	56.7
responsive	17.6	15.4	16.7
Gubernatorial role in fundraising			
little or none	29.4	0.0	16.7
responds to requests	58.8	61.5	60.0
active fundraiser	11.8	38.5	23.3

An Index of Party-Governor Linkage

A summary index of state party-gubernatorial linkage was derived from the measures shown in Table 6.1. First, separate indices were constructed for organizational involvement in gubernatorial affairs and for gubernatorial involvement in party affairs. These two indices were then summed to create a single index measure of the total level of interaction.

This interaction index was then discounted for lack of reciprocity in the interactions. The linkage scores of nine of the 30 state parties were reduced because the pattern of interaction was predominantly one of gubernatorial involvement in party affairs without a corresponding party involvement in gubernatorial affairs. The most imbalanced state parties studied were the Texas Republicans and the West Virginia Democrats, both of which were heavily dominated by their governors. The median score on the resulting index (range $= 0 \rightarrow 6$) is 3.9, suggesting that state party organizations are at least moderately linked with their governors. Indeed, over one-third of the party organizations have a fairly high level of linkage (i.e., score of 5 or 6). There is a slight, but statistically insignificant, tendency for Republican state party organizations to be more highly linked with their governors than are the Democrats (though we have noted above qualitative differences on the relationships).

High scores on this party-governor index should not be taken to imply strict parity of influence in party-gubernatorial relations. The highest scoring state parties are characterized by a high frequency of interaction with the governor (weekly meetings with governor), a high level of gubernatorial service to the party (e.g., involvement in recruitment, fundraising), and a high level of gubernatorial demand upon the party organization. In most of these state parties, the organization defers to the governor. Nevertheless, the *raison d'etre* of the party organization extends far beyond the reelection of the governor. State party organizations with high levels of linkage are not unquestioningly compliant to the governor. For example, a midwestern Democratic chair, whose party is noted for its firm ideological commitments, reported that he regularly consulted with the governor, but added, "we have our own policies." And in many states where linkage is high, the state chair was selected through competitive elections, not through designation by the governor. In the prevailing pattern of linkage, governors respond to state party initiatives but do not actively direct the party organization. High linkage levels usually result from a congruence of interests, a mutual interdependence, and a mutual willingness to accommodate.

The patterns associated with low party-governor linkage are much more varied. In some states, linkage is low because of a close relationship of the state party to some other officeholder (e.g., a U.S. senator). In other states, a moribund party organization provides little basis for interaction. Of course, some governors are elected as anti-party mavericks. In such instances, peaceful coexistence may express a high standard for gubernatorial party relations. Alternatively, as in Wisconsin after 1978, a maverick governor may seek to play a constructive role in the affairs of the party organization that opposed his/her nomination. For some governors, the party organization is relevant chiefly as a competitor for funds and animosity may result. Governors King of Massachusetts (1979–1982) and Brown of California (1974–1982) illustrate this pattern of competitive relations tinged by animosity. In a few instances, state party leaders view close links with the governor as potentially destructive to the party organization. Thus, there are greater qualitative differences among those state parties characterized by low linkage with the governor than among the parties with high levels of linkage.

Party and Legislators

We have already seen that it can be misleading to compartmentalize analysis of the relations between the state party organization and the governor and legislature. Gubernatorial relations with the party may be instrumental to the governor's legislative purposes, and the quality of the state party's relations with members of the legislature may have a bearing on its dealings with the governor. Indeed, for a perennially minority party, the salience of party in the legislature may be crystallized by the party's success in electing a governor. But there are also a number of factors that distinguish analysis of state party relations with the legislature:

1. The party is present in the legislature not merely as a subjective orientation of the members, but also as an organization. The formal legislative party leadership structures, which frequently are staffed, conduce to state party-legislative party contacts.
2. Some state chairs are concurrently members of the legislature and 30 percent have had legislative experience.[4] Thus, party-legislative linkage may be facilitated by the career patterns of some chairs.
3. While the party either has or does not have the governorship, the party position in the legislature is measured on a continuous scale. With few exceptions, it is meaningful to ask whether a party holds a majority or minority of the legislative seats, and which party has organized the legislature.[5] When the perennial representation of one party in the legislature approaches zero, these questions, which assume party competition and the possibility of shifting control, lose much of their significance.

TABLE 6.2.
The Linkage of State Party Organizations with State Legislators by Percentages of Parties (27 sample states, 1979–1980).

	Democrats	Republicans	Total
Types of interactions			
internal party affairs	26.9	48.1	37.7
electoral & constituency affairs	30.8	66.7	49.1
public policy	76.9	51.9	64.2
none	11.5	7.4	9.4
Frequency of interactions			
little/none	7.7	25.9	17.0
some	57.7	29.6	43.4
a good deal	34.6	44.4	39.6
Overall integration			
none	11.5	7.4	9.4
low	23.1	22.2	22.6
moderate	50.0	33.3	41.5
high	15.4	37.0	26.4

4. Recruitment and support of legislative candidates is one of the concerns of state party organizations. Such activity should facilitate state party access to the legislators. But the legislators come from local constituencies and it seems likely that local parties will have greater claims of access to the legislators. The state party must attempt to benefit rather than be hurt by this pattern of localized legislative access. Thus, in addition to building bridges to the legislators through campaign assistance, the state party may enhance linkage to the legislators through strengthening its integration with the local parties. For these reasons, party-legislative linkage will differ from party-governor linkage.

Measuring Linkage with Legislators

While the concept of linkage, with its emphasis upon interdependence and reciprocity, is applicable to party relations to legislators as well as to governors, the major disparities between the two offices require that the specific measure for legislative linkage vary from those for gubernatorial linkage. Parties interact with their state legislators on matters relating to (1) internal party affairs, (2) electoral and constituency affairs, and (3) policy matters. Table 6.2 reports the frequency of the various types of interactions.

Substantial differences exist in the patterns of Democratic and Republican interaction with the legislators. Democratic state party organizations tend to deal with state legislators on public policy matters much more than do Republicans, although most state parties do relate to legislators on policy matters. Furthermore, nearly three-fifths of the Democrats reporting policy contacts, and just over two-fifths of the Republicans, indicate that such contacts include party and electoral policy in their scope. It was more usual for chairs in each party to contact legislators on changes in electoral law than on other policy concerns. If the Democrats had the edge on policy contacts, Republican chairs, to a greater extent than Democrats, reported legislative party contacts dealing with internal party affairs such as party-building programs, and covering electoral and constituency matters.

While Table 6.2 shows that more state Republican organizations deal with legislators on a wider array of matters than do Democrats, it also shows a much higher incidence among Republican chairs of reporting little or no frequency of interaction with legislators. The seven Republican state organizations showing little relationship to their state legislators are in Florida, Louisiana, Mississippi, Oregon, Rhode Island, Texas, and Virginia. Only in Florida and Oregon did Republican strength exceed 25 percent of the seats in one or both chambers of the legislature at the time of this study. The other five states averaged seven percent in the upper chamber and 13 percent in the lower. It is not surprising to discover that the parties with little legislative contact also, as a rule, have few legislators to contact and little expectation of results from such contacts. The Democratic organizations with little or no legislative interaction were in California and Utah, where their substantial legislative representation suggests that other contextual factors may be related.

ORGANIZATIONAL DETERMINANTS OF PARTY-GOVERNMENT LINKAGE

Party Linkage with the Governor

Generally, it is expected that strong state parties will be better linked with their governors because the utility of the party is simply too great to ignore. Strong parties command resources that can be converted into influence-enhancing linkage. Within the context of this research, strong parties are those having strong and well-integrated state and local organizations. Consequently, we hypothesize that these party attributes are related to party-governor linkage.[6]

A curvilinear relationship is expected between the strength of party organizations and linkage with the governor. Weak parties lack resources to pursue linkage as defined here, and probably have little to attract gubernatorial overtures. In any event, such overtures, whether altruistic in motive and aimed at party building, or designed to make a personalized instrument of the party, would be short on the reciprocal element that is integral to our conception of linkage. Presumably, weak parties that are building will show increments in the strength of linkage which are related to increments of party organizational strength. But we are unable to test a hypothesis relating party organizational development to changing levels of linkage, and must restrict the analysis to a comparative assessment of the linkage experience of parties at varying levels of strength.

Party organizations of moderate strength have the incentive (in terms of building their constituencies and influence) and the resources to permit them to pursue linkage with the governor. At the same time, such parties are likely to be perceived by the governor as immediately or potentially useful. The strongest party organizations will have developed programs and priorities to which they are committed and hence will have also developed a sense of autonomous purpose. A party operating year-round, with a substantial budget and staff, although committed to winning the governorship and maintaining adequate relations with the party incumbent, will have other high-order goals to serve, which may sometimes distract from or conflict with the pursuit of gubernatorial linkage. They will also have diversified their constituencies by creating and satisfying the expectations of other party elites (party units, organizational activists, and a gamut of candidates and officeholders). Consequently, beyond some threshold, increments in party organizational strength may detract from linkage with the governor.

Figures 6.1, 6.2, and 6.3 present data relevant to these expectations. The horizontal axes represent degrees of the three dimensions of state party strength, state party and local party organizational strength and party integration, while the vertical axes represent levels of gubernatorial linkage. The curves on these figures result from a cubic regression of linkage on strength.[7] For the impact of state party strength on linkage with the governor, the data are remarkably consistent with the expectations. At low levels of organizational strength (less than -1 on the strength scale), linkage is low and increments in strength are associated with increase in linkage, but only to a certain level or threshold. Beyond this, additional strength is associated with declining levels of linkage. This threshold may represent the point at which the party organizations have become sufficiently strong to differentiate themselves, and at which the organizations have developed goals and alliances detracting from their concern for the governorship. The party's capacity for action does not constitute a threat or enough of a potential

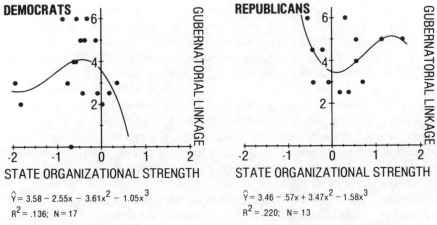

$\hat{Y} = 3.58 - 2.55x - 3.61x^2 - 1.05x^3$
$R^2 = .136;\ N = 17$

$\hat{Y} = 3.46 - .57x + 3.47x^2 - 1.58x^3$
$R^2 = .220;\ N = 13$

FIGURE 6.1. State Party Organizational Strength and Gubernatorial Linkage.

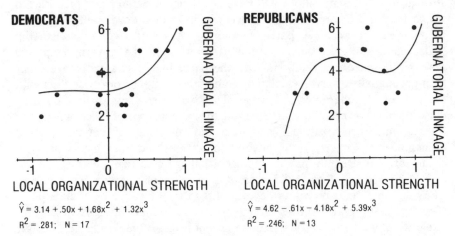

$\hat{Y} = 3.14 + .50x + 1.68x^2 + 1.32x^3$
$R^2 = .281;\ N = 17$

$\hat{Y} = 4.62 - .61x - 4.18x^2 + 5.39x^3$
$R^2 = .246;\ N = 13$

FIGURE 6.2. Local Party Organizational Strength and State Party Linkage with Governors.

resource to the governor to warrant giving it special attention. However, when the party organization moves out of this intermediate zone to a higher plateau of strength (greater than + 1), the organization is capable of commanding the governor's attention and hence strength contributes to linkage. These interpretations must be treated as only suggestive because of the small number of cases, the lack of control variables, and uncertainty about the appropriateness of generalizing from the high and low strength ranges that are actually party-specific. Nevertheless, the data are compatible

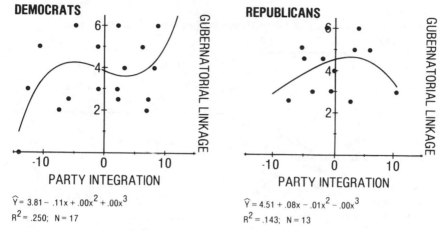

FIGURE 6.3. Integration of Party Units and Party Linkage with Governors.

with an understanding of party-governor relations that posits motives and capabilities for interaction that change as the organizational strength of the party changes.

The attractiveness of the state party as an object of linkage should be enhanced for the governor when local parties in the state are also strong, and when the state and local parties are well integrated. When local organizations are strong they are attractive as vote-mobilizing agents, and because they are numerous, a strong party organization is perceived by the governor as a convenient coordinating mechanism. Thus, strong local party organization can induce the governor to turn to the state party for help in exploiting their electoral potential,[8] and strong state-local party integration should add to that inducement. As with state party organizational strength, we expect that the relationships will be curvilinear, since the constituency commitment and party organizational interests of the stronger local parties will have a flattening impact on their incentive for linkage.

The data presented in Figure 6.2 are not only consistent with these expectations for the impact of local party strength on linkage, but they are also consistent with the relationship observed between state party organizational strength and party-governor linkage.[9] That is, increments in local party strength enhance state party linkage when the local organizations are initially weak (for Republicans only) or when they have achieved significant organizational strength (for both Republicans and Democrats). Thus, a similar process seems to effect the translation of state and local strength into state party linkage with the governor.

The impact of party integration upon state party linkage with the governor is more party specific than that of local party strength. As Figure

TABLE 6.3.
A Multivariate Analysis of Party-Governor Linkage (27 sample states, 1979-1980).

	Democrats		Republicans	
	Cumulative R^2	$\bar{R}^2$	Cumulative R^2	$\bar{R}^2$
State organizational strength State organizational strength^2 State organizational strength^3	.136	−.064	.220	−.039
Local organizational strength Local organizational strength^2 Local organizational strength^3	.432	.092	.695	.391
Party integration Party integration^2 Party integration^3	.570	.141	.709	.126

$\bar{R}^2$ = adjusted R^2
Note: See footnote 7.

6.3 demonstrates, the integration of local Republican organizations with the state organization does not substantially enhance state party linkage with the governor ($R^2 < .20$). The relationship is stronger for Democrats, however, with increments in party integration having the greatest impact on party-governor linkage when party integration is either low or high. As with party organizational strength, the relationship flattens out at moderate levels of party integration. This may reflect the tendency of organizations at a certain state of development to be concerned more with organization-building than with external relationships. Except at this stage, greater intraparty coordination contributes to party-governor linkage.

In the bivariate analysis of the contribution of local party strength to party-governor linkage, we assumed that local party organizational strength is relevant to state party relations with the governor only to the extent that the parties are highly integrated. In order to test more explicitly this assumption, it is necessary to explore the interrelationships of local strength and integration through a multivariate analysis. Table 6.3 reports the results of regressing party-governor integration on measures of state strength, local strength, and party integration. It can be seen that for both parties, local organizational strength is the most significant explanatory factor, possibly supporting the adage that even statewide elections are local elections requiring local organizational resources.

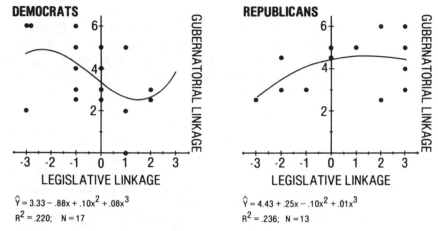

$$\hat{Y} = 3.33 - .88x + .10x^2 + .08x^3$$
$$R^2 = .220; \quad N = 17$$

$$\hat{Y} = 4.43 + .25x - .10x^2 + .01x^3$$
$$R^2 = .236; \quad N = 13$$

FIGURE 6.4. Party-Legislative Linkage in Relation to Party-Governor Linkage.

Since there is reason to believe that one of the principal services that governors want from the state party is assistance in securing legislative support for their programs, it follows that a party with good linkage to its partisans in the legislature has more to offer a governor, than a party with weak or nonexistant legislative relations. Hence, we encroach upon the legislative linkage analysis of the next section of this chapter by seeking to answer the question whether high party-legislative linkage enhances the state party's linkage with the governor. The data relevant to this question is shown in Figure 6.4.

Contrary to our expectations, the slope of the relationship for Democratic parties is primarily negative. That is, as legislative linkage increases, gubernatorial linkage decreases. This relationship is clearest at moderate levels of legislative linkage, and could reflect the parties' responses to the recent tendency of governors and gubernatorial candidates to pursue their electoral interests through non-party organizations. However, because of the small number of Democratic parties that have achieved even a moderate level of linkage with their state legislative leadership, we are not very confident in rejecting the hypothesis.

The Republican pattern is substantially different. The Republican slope is positive, in conformity with the hypothesis, and many more Republican parties have achieved high linkage with their state legislative leadership. For Republicans, increases in linkage with the state legislature do enhance party linkage with the governor. There is no tendency among the Republicans toward the offsetting of low gubernatorial linkage with high legislative linkage, as was suggested by the Democratic data. This may reflect the significantly different resource levels of the parties. For the Democrats, chronic resource shortages may compel the allocation of support in a more selective way. As is discussed more fully in the next section, greater Republican resources may enable them to pursue linkages with both legislators and the governor simultaneously.

Party Linkage with Legislators

As with party linkage with the governor, we expect that party-legislative linkage will be a function of organizational attributes, namely the organizational strength of the state and local parties, and the level of integration of the two. However, it is quite unlikely that for the Democrats, legislative linkage will parallel the gubernatorial linkage pattern which we found in the preceding section. In testing for the impact of state party legislative linkage on linkage with the governor, we found a negative relationship ($r = -.45$) for the Democrats. Where Democratic state party legislative linkage is high, linkage with the governor tends to be low. For the Republicans, legislative linkage is positively associated with gubernatorial linkage ($r = +.40$). While Democratic parties may perceive gubernatorial and legislative linkage as alternative strategies for the party, Republican parties appear to find the two types of linkage compatible. Consequently, we expect the correlates of Republican legislative linkage to be similar to the correlates of Republican gubernatorial linkage.

The data relevant to the relationships between state and local party organizational strength, state-local party integration, and state party linkage with the governor are presented in Figures 6.5, 6.6, and 6.7. The Democratic portion of Figure 6.5 which shows the relationship between party organizational strength and legislative linkage is the inverse of the Democratic portion of Figure 6.1. Beyond a threshold of moderate organizational strength, parties have little to offer candidates or officeholders, and they also pose little threat as competitors for scarce resources and influence. As the weak organization acquires strength, the most effective strategy for resource allocation may be to focus on the principal political office in the state. Such a strategy is unlikely to contribute to a close rapport between the party organization and those who are excluded from party support. Beyond some threshold level of strength, it becomes feasible for the party organization to operate on a broader electoral front, extending assistance to legislators as well. Because Democratic organizations so rarely achieve levels of strength sufficient to pursue gubernatorial and legislative linkage at equal levels, party resource allocation takes on a zero-sum quality.

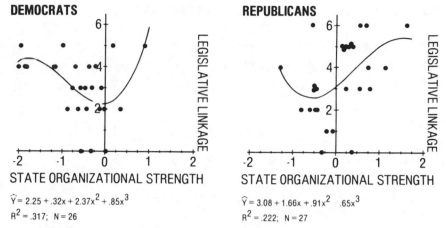

FIGURE 6.5. State Party Organizational Strength and Party-Legislative Linkage.

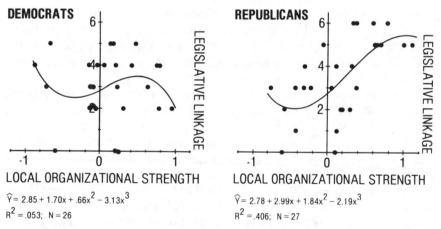

FIGURE 6.6. Local Party Strength and State Party Linkage with the Legislature.

Quite in contrast, Republicans do not seem to experience this kind of conflict. The Republican portions of Figures 6.1 and 6.5 are strikingly similar. Republican linkage with both legislators and governor increase sharply with increments in strength beyond the moderate level. Short of this level, increments in strength are associated with decreasing levels of linkage. This contrast between Democratic and Republican linkage patterns becomes more apparent when legislative linkage scores for parties controlling the

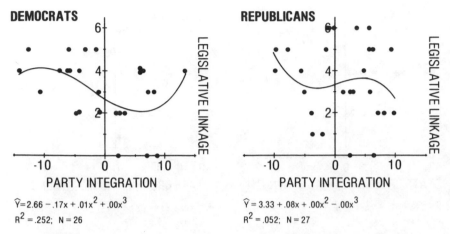

FIGURE 6.7. Integration of Party Units and Party Linkage with the Legislature.

governorship and parties which do not are compared. Under these alternative conditions, levels of Republican linkage with the state legislature do not differ significantly. For the Democrats, legislative linkage is substantially higher for parties that do not control the governorship, a finding that supports our understanding of gubernatorial and legislative linkage as alternative strategies for Democrats.

On the impact of local party strength on state party linkage to the governor, the patterns are again quite different for the two parties. Local party strength for the Democrats, contrary to our expectations, does not enhance state party linkage with the legislators (see Figure 6.6). Indeed, there is virtually no relationship. For Republicans the contrary is true with increments in local party strength associated with increments in state party linkage with the legislators. Again, this curve replicates the Republican curve for gubernatorial linkage in Figure 6.2 and is consonant with the analysis given for Figure 6.4. Republicans, but not Democrats, may be able to rely on local party resources for building a relationship with their legislative contingent.

For Democrats, the relationship between party integration and state party-legislative linkage is substantial but not in the expected direction. As Figure 6.7 shows, increments in party integration are generally associated with decrements in party-legislative relations. For Republicans, party integration has no impact. That party integration would detract from party-legislative linkage for Democrats is paradoxical. Where state parties are relatively weak and local parties strong, shared or integrated resources may better serve the interests of the local party than the objectives of the state party. Consequently, increases in party integration do not assist the state

TABLE 6.4.
A Multivariate Analysis of Party-Legislative Linkage (27 sample states, 1979–1980).

	Democrats		Republicans	
	Cumulative R^2	$\bar{R}^2$	Cumulative R^2	$\bar{R}^2$
State organizational strength State organizational strength^2 State organizational strength^3	.317	.224	.222	.120
Local organizational strength Local organizational strength^2 Local organizational strength^3	.360	.157	.547	.412
Intra-party integration Intra-party integration^2 Intra-party integration^3	.531	.311	.548	.347

$\bar{R}^2$ = adjusted R^2

Note: See footnote 7.

party in its relationship with the state legislature. Generally, for neither party does the analysis of the impact of party integration on state legislative linkage support the hypothesis. When the legislative integration scores are subjected to multivariate analysis (see Table 6.4), the Republican pattern is seen to be quite similar to that observed in the case of party-governor integration. That is, the most significant predictor of party-legislative linkage is the strength of local party organizations, followed by the strength of the state party organizations. The contribution of levels of party integration to the prediction of levels of party-legislature linkage is slight. On the other hand, the Democratic results for state legislative linkage vary somewhat from the findings for gubernatorial linkage. The most useful predictor of levels of state legislative linkage is the strength of the state party, while local party strength is of little predictive utility. Nevertheless, levels of party integration contribute substantially to levels of legislative linkage. Where local parties are integrated (irrespective of whether the local parties are strong or weak), Democratic state parties are more successful at achieving linkage with the legislative leadership. For the Republicans, local organizational strength contributes to state party-legislative linkage regardless of the level of integration with the state party. Democratic party integration contributes to party-legislative linkage without regard to levels of local party strength. We think that party differences in program emphasis and extent of reliance upon non-party groups may account for the differential impact of party integration on linkage with legislative leaders. The Democratic emphasis upon vote mobilization, and the need to coordinate the activities of non-party groups, may heighten the significance of relationships between different levels of party for relationships between the state party and legislators.

Linkage as a Function of Organization

Three conclusions emerge from this discussion. The first is that the state parties have the organizational capacity to achieve linkage, and do in fact relate to governors and legislators in significant degree and on a variety of consequential matters. Second, and of greatest significance, dimensions of state party organizational strength clearly influence the level of party linkage with officeholders. Third, there are party differences on patterns of linkage and on the association of organizational strength with linkage.

State parties have several interests in pursuing linkages with governors and legislators. These include patronage, giving and receiving help with candidate recruitment, campaigning, and fund raising, and influencing public policy, especially electoral law. Seventy percent of the state parties report some level of involvement in state patronage. Nearly three-quarters of them are assisted by their governors in candidate recruitment, and a similar proportion benefit from gubernatorial fundraising assistance. Three-quarters of the chairs report the organization provided campaign services to their governors as candidates, and just under half made financial contributions to the gubernatorial campaign. These are activities which, directed at candidates, should facilitate party access to the elected officeholder. Even if today it is not thought that state party organizations have much opportunity to play an active role in governmental activities, there is substantial evidence of the interest that governors have in influencing party affairs. Forty-three percent of the party chairs report the governor played an instrumental role in their selection and just over half thought it necessary to have the governor's support before acting on some matters. Only ten percent of the chairs asserted the governor had little or no relationship to the party organization.

All of these relationships vary by party, some substantially, but not in a consistent direction. Twice as many Republican organizations contributed $50,000 or more to the gubernatorial campaign than did the Democrats. Democratic governors, on the other hand, exert much stronger influence in the selection of state chairs than do Republicans. Nearly 30 percent of the Democratic chairs think it important to be spokesperson for the governor, while no Republicans place such emphasis on this role. Republican governors who are rated as active fundraisers outnumber the Democratic governors in that category by more than three-to-one.

The state party relates to its legislative leadership on party affairs, election and constituency affairs, and on substantive policy matters, especially election law. The strength of relationships that directly involve or clearly imply a policy interest is surprising at first, but perhaps should be read in the context of gubernatorial reliance on party for help with the legislative program. Over three-quarters of the Democratic chairs and over half of the Republicans report such contacts. Eighty-three percent of the party chairs report a good deal of interaction with their state legislative leaders, but here too, there are significant party differences, with three times as many Republicans (26 percent) reporting little or no interaction as Democrats (8 percent).

We also find party differences in the relationships between party organizational attributes and party-government linkage. The generally stronger Republican organizations have a capacity to pursue simultaneous relations with both the governor and legislature, while the weaker Democrats find it necessary to choose one or the other. Local organizational strength seems to have a similar effect. While these relationships are sometimes complex, they are clear in arguing that party organizational attributes structure in important ways party linkages with the party-in-government.

NOTES

1. "When Key used the term 'linkage' in 1961, it was little more than plain speech; he asked how governmental action and public opinion are linked. As a synonym for 'interrelated,' or as an alternative way of noting 'interdependence,' or even as a proxy term for referring obliquely to reciprocal 'influences,' to say that things were 'linked' must have seemed a straightforward, unpretentious, and innocuous way to make his points to readers put off by social-science jargon" (Marvick, 1980, p. 108).

2. In Chapter 2 we offered data on party programs which have the capacity to influence the electorate. In Chapter 5 we test hypotheses relating party organizational strength to levels of interparty competition and of electoral success in party contests for public office. Thus, with the concern in Chapter 6 for party relations with officeholders, we have ranged over the full territory, from electorate to officeholders, contemplated by Key as being within the province of linkage. But we should stress that we have not examined party relations with the electorate within a linkage model. The conceptual focus for our study is party organizational strength, and the theoretical emphasis is upon the determinants and consequences of party organizational strength.

3. Of 53 state chairs interviewed, 27 were currently serving with governors of the same party and an additional three chairs had served with a predecessor governor.

4. Eight state party chairs interviewed were or had recently been members of the state legislature, three in the lower house and five in the upper. Six were Democrats and two Republicans. The eight constitute a non-negligible segment (15 percent) of the 53 chairs interviewed. State legislator is the office target preferred and most frequently achieved by former state chairs (Huckshorn, et al., 1982a, Table VIII, p. 32).

5. The unicameral, nonpartisan Nebraska legislature provides one exception, another is the lower house of the Texas legislature which traditionally divides into a "Speaker's party" and an "anti-Speaker's party" to contest leadership positions. And, elsewhere in this chapter, we raise questions about the meaningfulness of speaking in terms of party competition in legislative bodies in which one of the two "major" parties holds 10 percent or less of the seats.

6. Organizational strength is but one way of reckoning a party's renomination significance to a governor. Morehouse (1980, 1981) measures this significance in terms of a party's durable capacity to register high primary votes for the winning nominee for governor. Application of this measure results in marked interparty differences with all but six state Republican parties falling within the strong-to-moderate range, and 21 of the Democratic parties coming within the weak range. Morehouse thinks that the lower ranges of primary plurality victories denote a party whose internal rivalries will not provide an incumbent governor with much support. The higher ranges indicate a party that has much to offer a governor by way of renomination support. However, we find no empirical relationship between our POS measure and Morehouse's measure.

7. A few comments on our statistical approach to the data will assist the reader in following the analysis. For simplicity's sake, we have utilized a cubic regression equation ($Y = a + bX + bX^2 + bX^3$) to analyze all of the bivariate relationships. The cubic equation allows a curvilinear relationship to emerge, but does not preordain that the relationship will be curvilinear (i.e., the coefficients for the quadratic and cubic terms could be empirically established to be zero). On theoretical grounds we expect many of the relationships under consideration to be curvilinear. In order that the analysis be comparable across parties and variables, the cubic regression line is reported for all analyses. Even if the incremental explained variance is minimal the quadratic and cubic terms have been forced into the equation. To reiterate, if these variables are not useful predictors of Y then their slopes will approach zero. The only negative aspect of this approach is that the degrees of freedom is reduced, although we do not use or report inferential statistics. Finally, the regression lines are still reported even when R^2 is low. When less than 20 percent of the variance in Y is explained by the cubic equation, we devote little attention to the functional form of the relationship. The 20 percent figure was established because the introduction of additional variables into regression equations always increases R^2. However, to require that each of the terms in the cubic equation explain at least 10 percent of the variance (for a cumulative standard of 30 percent) is far too rigorous a standard. Thus, it can be seen that most of our attention is devoted to interpreting the form of the relationships which exist, rather than trying to maximize explained variance.

8. We must acknowledge the existence of some county parties which, in effect, subsume the state party organization, and so recognize the occasional circumstance in

which the governor of the dominant party might work directly with the county party, and perhaps through it, with the state party.

9. This consistency is more readily apparent because at the local level the full range of variation in the organizational strength of both parties is represented in the data. Were the curves depicting the relationship between state strength and linkage generalized across party, the composite curve would be very similar to the ones depicted in Figure 6.2. Of course, care must be exercised in interpreting these data because of the small number of cases, and because Republican organizations are on average significantly stronger than Democratic organizations. Thus, some of the apparent differences in the curves in these figures is attributable to discrepancies in the strength of Republican and Democratic organizations. And since we observe very few weak Republican organizations and few strong Democratic organizations, the range of experience at the ends of the continuum are specific to each party.

7

The Changing Environment of Party Organizations

American students of party have leaned toward "an exaltation of their subject matter . . . a belief in a nearly overwhelming importance of parties in the modern political process" (Epstein, 1980, p. 7). This has been expressed in hyperbole about parties as "makers of democratic government" (Schattschneider, 1942, p. 1), and in prescriptions for the parties to institute "responsible party government" (APSA Committeee, 1950). There is a tendency to evaluate parties against performance standards which impute to party "primacy" or a role as "causes rather than effects" (Sorauf, 1980, p. 410). With modest expectations, and with findings which are sometimes strong, sometimes weak, and sometimes mixed, we have examined the party organizations as "independent rather than dependent variables" (Sorauf, 1980, p. 410) in relation to party integration, electoral success, and linkage with officeholders. But parties are also acted upon and to at least some extent may be expected to be creatures of their environments. In this chapter we examine three sources of influence on the parties as organizations: public policy, the competitive influence of extra-party organizations in a rapidly changing electoral environment, and the attitudes or role orientations of party organizational elites.

Public Policy on Parties

Traditionally viewed as voluntary associations inherently extra-legal in nature (Horn, 1956, p. 99; Schattschneider, 1942, pp. 11–12), American parties are now generally conceded to be the most regulated in the world (Epstein, 1980, p. 44). This was the case long before Congress and the state legislatures in the mid-1960s embarked on a course which has increased the

131

variety and incidence of legislation on parties and campaigns, with profound impact upon the relation between parties, candidates, and other participants in electoral politics. Although descriptive studies and compilations of state laws pertaining to party "membership," candidacy, ballot access, and the structure and management of parties appeared at frequent intervals,[1] little consideration was given to possible causal relationships between law and party until the late 1960s.

That research focused upon deterrents to voting and the effects of institutional arrangements for registering and counting votes upon the allocation of seats in the legislature. Douglas Rae's seminal book on *The Political Consequences of Electoral Laws* (1967) carves out for study laws "which govern the processes by which electoral preferences are articulated as votes and by which these votes are translated into distributions of . . . parliamentary seats . . . among the competing political parties" (p. 14). Also publishing in 1967, Kelley and associates pushed the analysis to an earlier point in the electoral cycle, examining the deterrent effects of registration requirements on registration and voting in 104 cities. Rosenstone and Wolfinger (1978, p. 41), assessing the relationship of registration laws to turnout, concluded that "if every state had registration laws as permissive as those in the most permissive states, turnout would have been about nine percentage points higher in the presidential election" of that year. Kousser (1974) established, and Rusk (1974) and Rusk and Stucker (1978) elaborated on the success of restrictive legislation in suppressing black voting and depressing suffrage levels in the South. In 1970, Rusk convincingly argued that the introduction of Australian ballot laws in the American states in the last decades of the nineteenth century stimulated a large increase in split-ticket voting. But, while there is a growing tradition of concern for public policy, no systematic effort has been made to assess the impact of public policy on party organizations.

The burgeoning of new legislation has generated considerable speculative interest in the consequences of such legislation for party organizations. Some political scientists believe the new patterns of legislation are harmful to the political parties (Kirkpatrick, 1978; Ranney, 1975). On the other hand, Gordon Black (1975, pp. 12–13) considers that "the new campaign laws operate to enhance the power and influence of the state and national committees within both parties. . . . As organizations, the state and national party organizations enjoy a formidable set of advantages" under the new laws.

Today American parties are much more than at any time earlier in the 20th century, public instruments circumscribed by statutory and administrative regulation and supported by public funds. Of the 50 states, 18 have some form of campaign subsidies; eight of these direct the subsidies to campaign organizations, nine to party organizations, and one to both (Jones,

TABLE 7.1
Components of State Public Policy on Party.

Component	Weight
I. Support Mechanisms	
A. Facilitation of major party control over nominations and elections	10
B. Direct Party/candidate subsidies	5
C. Difficulty of achieving "major party" status	6
D. Allowance of non-partisan elections	4
E. Party role in staffing polls	2
II. Statutory Regulation	
A. Party structure/hierarchy	10
B. Leadership position attributes	4
C. State-substate integration	10
D. Restrictions on expenditures/revenues	6

1981). State subsidies to parties are occasionally justified as building stronger institutional parties and sharpening interparty competition, although to the extent that public policy subsidizes candidate campaign organizations, policy is widely seen as being debilitating to party organizations (e.g., Kirkpatrick, 1978). But the strength of party organizations may itself be important in structuring public policy. Party leaders can be effective lobbyists, and when the monopoly of the two major parties on the electoral apparatus is threatened, the major parties can form an indivisible trust. It might, therefore, be hypothesized that there is a reciprocal relationship between party organizational strength and public policy concerning parties.

We expect public policies supportive and regulative of party to stimulate party organizational strength. We recognize that the stimulus may in part lead to staffing party organizations with compliance specialists, and it may also dilute the resources devoted to candidate recruitment, campaign training, electorate mobilizing, and election-winning activities. Nevertheless, the party organizations are probably strengthened in their capacity to perform these tasks as well as to relate to candidates, other party organizations and political action committees (PACs). Since such legislation generally includes provisions defining the entitlement of party organizations to spend on the campaigns, these legal entitlements become performance norms that parties are expected to fulfill, thus stimulating activity. This is the reasoning that leads us to expect a strong relationship between supportive and regulatory policy on parties and party organizational strength.

In order to test for the expected relationships between dimensions of public policy and the strength of party organizations, it is necessary to construct a measure for public policy that incorporates both the regulatory and support aspects of such policy. The components of this measure are outlined in Table 7.1.

A basic conceptual distinction is made between statutory support mechanisms and statutory regulation. Support mechanisms are directly protective of the major party control of the political marketplace. For instance, the variable representing facilitation of control over nominations and elections is itself an index comprised of six variables including:

1. the openness of primaries;
2. the restrictiveness of regulations governing voter party declaration;
3. whether a straight-ticket option is provided to voters;
4. whether a "disaffiliation" statute exists (i.e., a statute requiring that independent presidential candidates and/or electors declare they are not members of any political party at some period of time prior to their nomination);
5. whether a "sore-loser" statute exists (i.e., a statute precluding a candidate who has lost the primary from running as an independent for the same office in the succeeding general election); and
6. whether the party has the authority to replace deceased or resigned candidates.

Statutes that provide parties with closed primaries, stringent regulations controlling declaration of party affiliation, the straight-ticket option, the means of punishing dissident candidates, and the authority to designate candidates under special circumstances, are providing very substantial direct benefits to the parties. When coupled with a high entry barrier to achieving the status of "major party," support mechanisms of this sort are possibly even more valuable than financial subsidies. Such barriers range from the quite rigorous Minnesota requirement that a party maintain an organization and receive at least five percent of the statewide vote (and some votes in every county) for a statewide candidate, to an absence of statutory definitions of party in Louisiana, where all candidates compete in a single primary ballot (Robeck et al., 1978). Using a theoretically derived system of weights, an index of supportiveness was devised.

As may be seen from Table 7.1, regulatory policy is measured in terms of four kinds of statutory provisions which seek to constrain aspects of party structure or the activities of party: (1) party structure and hierarchy, (2) leadership attributes (e.g., regulation of process of leadership selection), (3) state substate party organizational integration (e.g., extent to which substate party unit officials are members of state party governing structure), and (4) restrictions on expenditures and revenues. It is a dichotomous measure which indicates only the presence or absence of statutory regulation for these

TABLE 7.2.
State Scores on Public Policy on Party Support 1979–1980.

State	Score	State	Score
Wyoming	14.9*	Iowa	70.1
California	19.7	Montana	70.2
Wisconsin	23.6	Missouri	70.9
Kansas	24.7	New Mexico	71.0
Pennsylvania	31.2	Vermont	71.2
Massachusetts	33.6	Nevada	73.9
Nebraska	39.2	Arizona	80.0
Washington	41.9	North Dakota	82.1
Michigan	42.2	Rhode Island	86.2
Tennessee	42.8	Virginia	86.3
Louisiana	43.2	West Virginia	90.8
Mississippi	44.5	New Jersey	92.9
New Hampshire	48.0	Hawaii	94.1
South Carolina	49.4	Maryland	94.4
South Dakota	50.8	Illinois	95.0
Oklahoma	52.0	Colorado	98.2
Texas	53.2	Alabama	101.5
Delaware	56.0	North Carolina	101.8
Idaho	56.6	Alaska	102.9
Ohio	59.4	Florida	103.4
New York	61.5	Utah	109.9
Georgia	61.5	Oregon	113.3
Minnesota	62.2	Indiana	114.6
Arkansas	63.4	Maine	142.0
Connecticut	63.7	Kentucky	154.7[†]

*Least supportive.
[†] Most supportive.

items. Thus, it is not important whether statutes set the length of the state chair's term at one year, or two years, or four years, but rather that the term is set by law. A weighted index from the four measures was then constructed.

Because we wish to ask two questions about statutory policy and party organization strength, we have created separate support and regulatory indexes. Indeed, the supportive and regulatory scores are not even positively related ($r = -.19$) so it is important to consider each component of policy separately. Tables 7.2 and 7.3 show the scores of each of the states on the two components.

Using the measures of policy on parties, we find no cross-sectional relationship between statutory regulation or support mechanisms and party

TABLE 7.3.
State Scores on Public Policy on Party Regulation 1979–1980.

State	Score	State	Score
Alaska	30.0*	Arkansas	168.3
Alabama	35.0	Wyoming	170.0
New Mexico	40.0	Idaho	175.0
Nebraska	55.0	South Carolina	180.0
Florida	63.3	North Dakota	181.7
Nevada	68.3	Michigan	183.3
Oklahoma	70.0	Tennessee	183.3
Hawaii	70.0	New Hampshire	185.0
Virginia	75.0	Vermont	185.3
New York	83.3	Utah	188.3
Connecticut	85.0	Washington	190.0
Georgia	85.0	South Dakota	200.0
Maine	90.0	Oregon	203.3
Missouri	90.0	Iowa	205.0
Texas	105.0	Arizona	205.0
Kentucky	105.0	Maryland	208.3
Mississippi	115.0	Colorado	208.3
North Carolina	120.0	California	210.0
Montana	125.0	Massachusetts	225.0
Rhode Island	136.7	New Jersey	230.0
Ohio	145.0	Wisconsin	231.7
Minnesota	145.0	West Virginia	238.3
Delaware	155.0	Illinois	250.0
Louisiana	155.0	Kansas	265.0
Pennsylvania	163.3	Indiana	270.0[†]

*Least regulatory
[†] Most regulatory

organizational strength in the late 1970s. In states in which public policy is more supportive and more regulatory of party, organizations are neither stronger nor weaker. However, we do find some relationship between supportive policy and increase in organizational strength for both parties. In states with supportive public policy, both Democratic and Republican organizations show greater increase in strength from the 1960s to the late 1970s than do parties in states with less supportive policies. These relationships are not strong (Democrats, $r = +.26$, Republicans, $r = +.32$), and there is a weak contrary trend for regulatory policy.

These state trends do not speak to federal trends (indeed, federal trends are not controlled in this analysis). We can assess neither the independent influence of national parties' rule changes on state party organizations, nor the effect of the Democratic reforms on the state policy measures that we employ. Further, a different mode of analysis is required to assess the role of state party organizations in this policy process, as well as whether the policies in question have differential impact on the parties (Jones, 1980). At a minimum, this analysis does suggest that law is not necessarily hazardous to the health of party organizations.

Organizations Competitive with Party in the Political Process

There is a widespread belief that as organizations other than parties seek to influence party nominations and to participate in campaigns for public office, their activities are necessarily threatening to the party organizations. Such extensions of activity from competitive organizations are assumed to constitute a kind of usurpation of party activities, and an absorption and expenditure of resources that might otherwise have gone to the party organizations. We do not make that assumption. Extra-party organizations, which in the form of PACs have spread like weeds under the beneficent provisions of the Federal Election Campaign Acts, may eventually put the parties out of business. However, if the party organizations adapt to the increasingly competitive organizational environment of politics, perhaps even finding ways to capitalize on the PAC phenomenon, they may actually profit rather than lose.

Because our framework for the study of state party organizations did not specifically include a major role for PACs operating at the state as well as national levels, we can make only a tentative contribution to the assessment of the impact of such organizations upon the party organizations. We did anticipate that the state party organizations would exhibit varying patterns of relationship to extra-party organizations within the state, and asked questions aimed at eliciting information on party relations with such groups. We draw upon these data in the brief analysis that follows.

We expect that extra-party organizations may differentially affect the two parties. That is, extra-party organizations may have a different relationship to the Republicans than to Democrats. It is easy to imagine, for instance, that labor organizations provide substantial financial support and voter mobilization activity to Democratic candidates, thus obviating the need of the party organization to provide such support (and resulting in Democratic organizations scoring lower on our party organizational strength scale). This line of reasoning leads to several important empirical questions, which can be addressed through our data. First, is there evidence of greater Democratic reliance on extra-party organizations? Second, do the state Democratic parties rely on different kinds of extra-party organizations than do the state Republican parties? Third, does the difference in types of extra-

TABLE 7.4.
Party Relations with Extra-Party Organizations (percent of chairs mentioning groups).

	Democrats	Republicans
Mentioning no extra-party organization	0	33
Mentioning a business, farm, or professional group	11	48
Mentioning a social action group	37	7
Mentioning a labor union	89	4
Mentioning a teachers group	41	4
Mentioning a party auxiliary group	0	15

$N = 27$ Sample State Republican Parties; 26 Sample State Democratic Parties (1979–1980).

party organizations supporting each party have implications for the nature and quantity of the assistance provided?

The data on which we rely to provide evidence relevant to these questions are derived from our interviews with the state chairs of the parties in 27 sample states. The state chairs were asked to indicate "What non-party groups in your state are closely aligned with the party and provide significant levels of assistance to the party and its candidates?" For each organization identified, they were further asked to indicate whether the organization provided assistance in fundraising, get-out-the-vote activity, research, and furnishing volunteers.

Table 7.4 reveals a striking difference between the two parties in their reliance upon extra-party organizational support. As expected, the Democrats are significantly more likely to report that they have such support than are the Republicans. None of the Democratic state chairs failed to claim such support, by contrast, one-third of the Republicans failed to mention such groups as sources of support. Differences in reliance on extra-party groups may explain in part, or be explained by, the consistent disparity between the parties in levels of organizational strength, and thus alternate causal patterns are possible. The Republicans may require strong organization in part because of low levels of support available from extra-party groups; alternatively, Republican strength may insulate it from such need and deter the party leaders from soliciting it. By contrast, the weaker Democratic state parties can normally anticipate that they will receive assistance from extra-party organizations, thereby compensating for their organizational disadvantage. This pattern of Republican reliance on the party organization is also reflected in the greater tendency of Republican than Democratic chairs to mention party auxiliary groups as sources of support.

There are also substantial differences in the types of organizations on which the two parties rely. The organizations mentioned by the state chairs were categorized as business, social action, labor, teachers, or party auxiliary. Almost 90 percent of the Democratic chairs mentioned receiving support from labor unions, and 41 percent noted that they had been supported by teachers' groups. If labor unions and teacher organizations are both considered as labor organizations, then every Democratic chair mentioned a labor group as providing assistance to the party. By contrast, only one of the Republican state chairs indicated that the party had received support from a labor union, and only one indicated teacher support. However, the prevalence of business support for the Republicans was not as great as that of union and teacher support for the Democrats. Almost half of the GOP chairs mentioned business group support, and 11 percent of the Democratic leaders acknowledged such support. The Democrats were much more likely to receive help from social action groups (e.g., blacks, Hispanics, feminists) than were the Republicans. As can be seen, the sources of party support, if not the levels of support from extra-party groups, are polarized.

Table 7.5 summarizes state chair reports of types of service received from extra-party organizations. Each party reports some external support in each of the service categories, with endorsing relegated to insignificance. State Democratic chairs mentioned 48 organizations providing assistance, and they display the heaviest reliance upon labor unions, with teachers and social action groups vying for second place. Republican chairs mention 21 groups, with clearly heavy reliance on business, farm, and professional sources of support. These data exclude multiple references by individual chairs to groups in a single category. Since we did not ask the chairs to estimate support levels for groups, we can make only the roughest comparison of the aggregate support which Democratic and Republican state parties received from extra-party groups. The effort to make such a comparison is aided by counting multiple responses by considering all reported incidents of receipt of service, including multiple reports of service from the same category of groups. These data are reported in Table 7.6. (By counting multiple responses, we increase the number of Republican mentions of business groups from 13 to 22 and of auxiliary party groups from 4 to 7; for the Democrats the number of social action groups is increased from 10 to 12.)

The data suggest that state Democratic parties receive relatively equal levels of support in three important areas: fundraising, volunteers, and efforts to get-out-the-vote. The Republican support is focused on fundraising, with volunteers the next closest level of support with only half the number of mentions as fundraising. Not unexpectedly, the Democrats also report two-and-a-half times the incidence of receipt of support from extra-party organizations as do the Republicans.

TABLE 7.5.
Services Provided by Extra-Party Organizations.

Type of Organization and Support Activity	Number of Groups Providing Support	
	Democrats	Republicans
Business, farm, professional		
Fundraising	3	12
Get-out-the-vote	1	3
Research	1	4
Volunteers	1	3
Endorsing	0	0
Total number of groups mentioned by state parties	3	13
Social action		
Fundraising	4	1
Get-out-the-vote	9	1
Research	3	0
Volunteers	8	1
Endorsing	1	0
Total number of groups	10	2
Labor unions		
Fundraising	23	1
Get-out-the-vote	19	0
Research	6	0
Volunteers	18	1
Endorsing	0	0
Total number of groups	24	1
Teacher groups		
Fundraising	9	1
Get-out-the-vote	7	0
Research	2	0
Volunteers	10	1
Endorsing	0	0
Total number of groups	11	1
Party auxiliary groups		
Fundraising	0	2
Get-out-the-vote	0	0
Research	0	1
Volunteers	0	3
Endorsing	0	1
Total number of groups	0	4

Note: In some instances the party leaders mentioned more than a single-specific group within the broader categories of groups. Even when the service was provided by more than a single group, it was counted only once.

$N = 27$ Sample State Republican Parties; 26 Sample State Democratic Parties (1979–1980).

TABLE 7.6.
Incidence of Service from Extra-Party Organizations

	Reported by	
Service	Democratic Chairs	Republican Chairs
Fundraising	40 (31%)	26 (51%)
Get-out-the-vote	37 (28%)	5 (10%)
Research	13 (10%)	7 (14%)
Volunteers	39 (30%)	12 (24%)
Endorsing	1 (01%)	1 (01%)
Totals	130 (100%)	51 (100%)

Multiple responses counted. When party leaders mentioned more than a single group within a category of groups multiple reporting of service in that category is counted.

$N = 27$ Sample State Republican Parties; 26 Sample State Democratic Parties, 1979–1980.

Our impressionistic conclusion from these data is that the two parties relate to extra-party organizations at the state level in just about the way that we would expect. The organizationally weaker Democratic parties draw upon such relationships to achieve combined activity levels that exceed those the party organization alone would be capable of mounting. The state Republican parties, generally stronger than the Democrats, exhibit less reliance upon external support of this kind and are accustomed to receiving a much more focused variety of support i.e., money from a much smaller number of organizations.

We think that in this sphere of organizational politics, and drawing no implications for the role of national political action committees, the question whether extra-party organizations are hurting or helping the parties is misphrased. The more appropriate question addresses the patterns of dovetailing and supplementing of party capacity and activity by extra-party organizations. The sources and kinds of support from such groups appear to reflect the electoral bases of the two parties and to respond to their organizational strengths and weaknesses.

The Impact of Leadership Role Orientations on Organizational Attributes of Party

In 1962, James Q. Wilson, noting that a new kind of politician had entered the scene, offered a dichotomized concept of descriptive utility that drew distinctions between the "professional" and the "amateur" in politics. The concept was immediately adopted by others as a theoretical variable and in the ensuing years a body of literature was built upon the Wilson conceptual foundation. The distinctions that he draws between the two types of political activists are based on: (1) a distinguishing pattern of cognitions and values; (2) certain demographic correlates; and (3) differing patterns of behavior.

The cognitions and values mark the strongly contrasting approach to party and politics that separate the amateur or "the new politician" from the professional or "the conventional politician" (Wilson, 1962, p. 9). The amateur emphasizes the role of ideas and principles in politics, is cosmo-politan, is policy-oriented, and sees parties as "sources of program and agents of social change." The professional scores low on all of these, and emphasizes interpersonal relations and the accommodation of interests. The professional tends toward parochialism, and has a high instrumental concern for party as a vehicle for winning office and providing rewards. Wilson finds amateurism associated with the demographic characteristics of youth, geographic mobility, professional occupations, unmarried status, being non-Catholic, middle or upper class, and well-educated. In reference to gender, Wilson confined himself to acknowledgment of the "active part" played by women in reform politics; others have emphasized the prominence of women in amateur politics (Kirkpatrick, 1976, p. 9; Epstein, 1980, p. 126).

Wilson acknowledged that his amateurs and professionals were ideal types and that in the real world the incidence of mixed types would be significant. He also recognized that political change and institutional imperatives might cause elites with professional cognitions and demographic attributes to take on the behavioral coloration of amateurs. "[F]ew amateurs act completely in accord with the logic of their position and many professionals have modified their behavior to keep pace with a changing political situation" (Wilson, 1962, p. 19). Costikyan (1966) narrates his ascent from reform district leader to Tammany chief in terms which raise the question whether amateurs may not be transmuted into professionals by the alchemy of politics. Thus we can readily imagine a continuum of amateurism ranging in commitment from strong to weak and in motive from clarity to ambivalence, to the point that mixed motive professionals and amateurs might be indistinguishable.

The rationale for expecting that amateurism among party leaders will have an impact on various dimensions of party organization is particularly appealing. Richard Hofstetter, for example, argues that group membership is determined by congruence between individual motives and group incentives (Hofstetter, 1973). This implies that a high incidence of amateurism among political activists should lead either to transference of that quality to the political organizations with which amateurs associate, or to the atrophy of political organization membership as amateurs keep distant from incongruent association. Jeane Kirkpatrick finds a large infusion of amateur and anti-organizational values and characteristics among delegates to national nominating conventions, particularly the Democratic convention of 1972, and concludes that the prominence of this "new breed" bodes ill for party organizations (Kirkpatrick, 1976, pp. 16–18). Her expectation is founded on the "assumption that an institution, such as a political party, lasts just as long as participants in that institution share expectations about what it should do and what they should do. When the understandings and goals of participants change, the institution changes" (p. 350). The values associated with a new breed of national nominating convention delegates are assumed predictive of the future of party organization, since the convention delegates of today are taken to be the party organizational leaders of the future. Kirkpatrick compares the party support scores of the 1972 Democratic Convention delegates and finds a precipitous decline from the scores for those who entered politics in the period 1960 to 1967, to those of delegates who entered politics in 1968 to 1972 (Table 5-4, p. 139). The consequences of such change are construed to be transforming and disruptive for the party organizations.

Analyses such as this have led to the perception that amateurism among party elites has profoundly negative consequences for the functioning of party organizations. Although it has been conventional to treat delegates as party leaders or at least representing the pool from which party leaders are chosen, we are not satisfied that this approach is empirically valid. Indeed, we believe that no dramatic change in party organizations should be expected as a consequence of change in the modal attitudes of convention delegates. There are three reasons for this expectation. First, the transfer of convention delegates' value-patterns to the state party organizational elites, either by concurrent state party officeholding by delegates or subsequent movement into state party office, is unlikely to occur at rates threatening organizational stability. Certainly if it is feasible to project a lagged relationship between convention delegates and the strength of state party institutions, it would be necessary to infer the condition of party from the values of those delegates who were most likely to be participant in state party organizations. Since Kirkpatrick accepts the prevalent view that national convention delegates no longer represent state party organizations (see Petrocik and Marvick, 1980, p. 4), but instead represent candidates (a view which is confirmed by Democratic Party rules) it is more sensible to attribute to candidate-oriented delegates a low incidence of pursuit of party office than to assume future office occupancy by this group with attendant effort to impose their anti-party views on the party organization. It is the party-oriented convention delegates who are most likely to participate in future party organizational activities and these probably have positive attitudes toward organization.

Second, processes of socialization of new leaders in the context of institutional values will, at the very least, moderate any predispositions toward anti-organizational behavior. The third reason is related to a problem inherent in the amateurism literature and recognized by Hofstetter (1973) and others, namely the tendency for any lack of precision in the conceptual classification to be exacerbated as it is operationalized to exclude a mixed category. The incidence of persons on the party office opportunity ladder who have mixed rather than pure amateur or professional attitudes is likely to be high, and this means that the number of dedicated amateurs seeking party office is probably quite low. Finally, whatever the values of its leaders, organizations are rarely perfectly malleable, thus the degree of organizational impact of amateurism must be considered an empirical question.

Before considering this question, however, it is useful to determine whether there has in fact been a noticeable infusion of amateurs into state party leadership positions. Table 7.7 reports the distribution of chair orientations over the two decade period from 1960 to 1980. The scores for the amateurism-professionalism orientations are derived from an index comprised of three standard items:

- Good party leaders must support any candidate nominated by the party even if they basically disagree with the candidate.
- Controversial positions should be avoided in a party platform in order to insure party unity.
- A gubernatorial candidate should not compromise on basic values even if such compromise is necessary to win.

Responses were recorded on a Likert response set. The upper portions of Table 7.7 report a variable which is the sum of the responses to the three items. A trichotomized version of this measure was created using the following categories: "primarily professional" (3–6), "mixed" (7–8), and "primarily amateur" (9–12). The distribution of this measure is shown in the lower portions of Table 7.7.

In considering the data on role orientation, two caveats should be kept in mind. First, it must be remembered that the orientations were measured on the basis of a 1978–1980 survey of former and contemporary state chairs and that these are not true panel data. Second, small Ns, particularly in the early periods, and relatively small differences in percentage distribution by orientation over time suggest caution in interpretation of the data.

When we do not allow for party differences, the data suggest there has been little change in the orientations of state party chairs over the period 1960 to 1980. There is no evidence of increasing amateurism among the state chairs, with the proportion of those holding amateur orientations holding steady at about one-fifth over the five periods into which the two decades are divided. The mixed category describes the greatest number of state party chairs in each of the periods. While it is usual to dichotomize the

TABLE 7.7.
Change in State Chair Role Orientations 1960–1980.

Role Orientation	Period			
	1960–1964	1965–1969	1970–1974	1975–1980
Democrats				
Mean[a]	7.3824	7.7000	7.7037	7.3538
Standard Deviation	1.2690	1.3229	1.5081	1.5755
N	17	25	27	65
Percent Professional	23.5	20.0	14.8	30.8
Percent Mixed	58.8	60.0	55.6	46.2
Percent Amateur	17.6	20.0	29.6	23.1
Republicans				
Mean[a]	7.1458	7.3529	7.1042	7.1235
Standard Deviation	1.4853	1.6215	1.4874	1.5422
N	24	34	48	81
Percent Professional	33.3	32.4	31.3	33.3
Percent Mixed	41.7	47.1	52.1	51.9
Percent Amateur	25.0	20.6	16.7	14.8

[a]Range: 3-12, with low scores indicating greater professionalism.

amateur-professional role orientations, Wilson presented these categories in terms of ideal types, and it is not surprising to find the chairs locating disproportionately in the mixed category when their responses are trichotomized. Professionalism has not declined over the 20-year period. Although the proportion of professionals declined slightly from 1960 to 1975, the contemporary period shows a somewhat higher ratio of professionals than in 1960–1964.

However, a different story emerges when we examine role orientations of state chairs by party. Fulfilling stereotypical expectations, the proportion of Democratic chairs in the amateur category has increased since 1960, while that of Republicans has decreased. Going against stereotype, the Republican proportion of amateur state chairs exceeded the Democratic in the first period (1960–1964), although it began a continuous decline in the next period. The Democratic proportion increased somewhat in the second period but did not pull significantly ahead of the Republican until 1970–1974, when it rose 10 points prior to falling off in the most recent period. We can only surmise the meaning of these contrasting trends. The relatively high levels of Republican amateurism in the first decade of the period studied could be accounted for by party-building. This was an era in which formerly dormant state parties were being revived, and party-building may well attract leaders exhibiting amateur values who emphasize ideology over material and solidary benefits derived from party work. The period from 1960 to 1964 followed eight years of rule and party-building effort by a Republican president who consistently sought to leaven the party organizations with amateurs (Cotter, 1983). It also witnessed a presidential candidacy in 1964 that is thought to have brought many amateur types into Republican organizational politics. For the Democrats, the ten-point rise in the percentage of amateur state chairs from the 1965–1969 period to 1970–1974 may be related to the inauguration of an era of Democratic party reforms following the 1968 Convention and to the 1972 McGovern presidential campaign. The coincidence of peak levels of amateurism with a "purist" presidential campaign for each of the parties is, at least, suggestive. John Kessel (1984, p. 77) calls attention to the high proportion of local campaign organization leaders who report they moved into such roles in presidential election years. Perhaps it is not inappropriate to speculate that "purist" presidential candidates might tend to attract like-minded persons to party leadership positions.

We should not be surprised at finding a stable proportion of professionals among the Republican chairs over the two decades, hovering at about one-third. While amateurs in the Democratic leadership positions have declined since 1970–1974, the most dramatic change to have occurred in the entire twenty-year period is the doubling of the proportion of professionals among Democratic chairs between the third and fourth periods. As Republican professionals held steady and amateurs declined, the mixed category of state party chairs has increased with near consistency over time. The Democrats have shown a nearly equivalent pattern of decrease in amateur leaders and, in the decade of the 1970s, a reversal of the proportions of amateurs and professionals. This shift, with the amateurs peaking in 1970–1974 and the professionals in 1975–1980, may parallel the changing course of the party struggle over reform.

We have seen (Chapter 2) that party organizational strength in the states has not declined over the two decades from 1960 to 1980 and, with some variation between the two parties, strength appears to have been markedly higher in 1980 than in 1960. When this trend is considered within the context of relative stasis in the distribution of state chair orientations over that period, no significant impact of orientations on strength should be expected. Yet these aggregate trends do not afford a conclusive test of the relationship. Instead, it is necessary to evaluate by party the degree of covariance between party leaders' orientations and organizational attributes. The specific hypothesis to be tested is that the orientations of the party leaders influence the structure and operations of the state party organizations. Since we can have greater confidence in the responses of state chairs

TABLE 7.8.
The Impact of Party Leader Orientations on State Party Structure, Program and Activity.

Organizational Attribute	Amateurism-Professionalism Orientations	
	Republicans	Democrats
Services to candidates	.18	−.09
Number of staff divisions	.19	−.23
Publication of a newsletter	.04	.08
Voter mobilization programs	.08	.01
Public opinion polling	−.17	.01
Headquarters accessibility	.08	.03
Candidate recruitment	.31	.03
Money contributions to candidates	.23	.19
Issue leadership	.26	.15
Size of staff	−.12	.07
Size of budget	−.12	−.05
Leadership professionalism	.02	−.03
Party organizational strength	.20	−.04

Note: Entries are Pearson correlation coefficients, based on the responses of 81 Republican state chairs and 65 Democratic state chairs serving in the period 1975–1980.

for the most recent of the four periods, and since the Ns for this group are suitably large, the hypothesis will be tested on this group of chairs only.

Table 7.8 shows the correlation between the role orientations of the state party leaders and the attributes of their party organizations. Generally, for Democrats there is virtually no relationship between chair orientations and any of the components of organizational strength. Amateurs and professionals both head up organizations with quite similar attributes. For Republicans, however, there are hints of at least a slight relationship with some of the component indicators. For instance, those with more amateurish chairs tend to recruit candidates for a wider range of offices ($r = .31$). There is also a slight tendency to distribute campaign money to more candidates. Perhaps more significantly, amateurism is associated with greater involvement in issue leadership. None of these relationships are strong, but the pattern of the correlations is interesting.

Generally, structural attributes of the organizations for both parties differ negligibly between organizations run by amateurs and those run by professionals. This finding is completely reasonable, although "professional" may sometimes be taken to imply a preference for a rational style of organization for the state party (in fact, the orientations are at least as relevant to ends as to means). It is easy to imagine that an ideologically inspired amateur would create or maintain a bureaucratized organization if such were deemed conducive to achieving ideological ends. After all, structure and ideology are entirely compatible within the communist parties of the world. Though amateur-led organizations may frequently be forced to rely on volunteers because of the absence of resources, it is not at all inconceivable that amateurs would prefer standardized and predictable organizational authority and procedures, clearly identified responsibilities, with structures that mirror functions, and the minimization of improvisation. On some of the less sophisticated measures of organizational strength, like size of budget and number of headquarters staff, amateur-professional differences are insignificant. It is not likely that amateurs are ideologically opposed to large budgets. Indeed, on these structural variables, to the extent that any differences at all exist, it is most likely that the differences stem from the availability of resources rather than the motivations of the party leaders.

It might be expected that greater differences exist on the activity variables. For instance, professionals are expected to emphasize institutional support activities while amateurs are expected to emphasize services to candidates. Insofar as parties support candidates, however, it might also be hypothesized that professionally led parties exhibit a stronger tendency toward universalistic programs available to all candidates, while amateur leaders apply an ideological litmus test in targeting programs and support to specific "acceptable" candidates. Thus, it is expected that services will be provided to a broader range of candidates when the state chair holds a more professional orientation.

As noted above, there is a correlation for the Republican organizations, however, it is not in the expected direction. Greater amateurism, rather than greater professionalism, is associated with greater involvement in recruiting and contributions to candidates for a larger variety of offices. Perhaps amateurs are more involved in recruitment out of a desire to seek out candidates who are "acceptable." Professionals have a strong interest in seeing that a full slate is put forth, but if the supply of candidates is ample, then not much effort may be required. Amateurs, on the other hand, may be more involved in recruitment and derecruitment; they encourage like-minded people to run and discourage those who are not like-minded. Thus, there is a higher level of amateur involvement in recruitment. Similarly, the professional organization may provide services more on the basis of need than on the basis of ideological criteria and that may account for the fact that the Republican amateur-led organizations provide money to candidates for a greater variety of types of offices than do professionally led organizations.

None of the relationships between state chair role orientations and attributes and activities of state party organizations is strong. Generally, there are only negligible organizational differences between parties run by chairs having amateur role orientations and parties headed by chairs expressing professional role orientations, and this is the case for both parties. In the light of the fact that strong party organizations can effectively serve the objectives of both types of party leader, this finding should not be surprising.

In general, the hypothesis that the role orientations of the state chairs have an impact on party organization must be rejected. Amateur, professional, and mixed orientations are compatible with a wide variety of party structures and activities. The only possible exception to this conclusion concerns state party integration with local parties; amateur state chairs lead somewhat better integrated parties. Generally organizational implications are slight.

Conclusion

In this chapter we have analyzed the impact on party organizational strength of public policy on party, extra-party organizations, and party leaders' role orientations. Although a compelling argument can be made for the proposition that public policy should significantly affect the condition of parties, this analysis has provided only a modest confirmation. No cross-sectional relationship was found between statutory support and regulatory measures with party organizational strength in the late 1970s. There was, however, a relationship between supportive public policy and an increase in party strength between the 1960s and 1980. Since the explosion of statutory enactments governing parties occurred during a period in which state parties generally experienced an increase in organizational strength, it would appear that at the very least the changes in public policy have not significantly damaged party organizations.

It should be noted, however, that public policy performs party maintenance functions. The law ordains that there shall be at least the shell of a party organization and generally invests the officers of this organization with functions of public significance. Public policy assures the minority party in the states of continued existence even at very low levels of electoral success. Stringent ballot access laws, for example, work to prevent the replacement of the minority party by new parties, and the consequent destabilizing of the existing party system. Therefore, public policy invests the two major parties with important systemic functions while protecting their longevity.

Although our data does not permit empirical testing of the impact of extra-party organizations on party organizational strength, we were able to identify significant differences between the Republicans and the Democrats in their relations with these groups. Democratic parties are much more likely to rely on extra-party organizations for assistance than are Republican organizations. Indeed, there was a marked tendency for the Republican state chairs to fail to mention any extra-party group as a source of assistance to the party or its candidates. The party support profiles differ as to the kinds of groups associated with each party (labor and teachers as principal sources of support for the Democrats and business groups for the Republicans), and the patterns of assistance received from these groups. We suggest that the patterns of group support parallel the patterns of electoral support for the two parties, and would appear to have the effect, if not the purpose, of compensating for disparity of organizational strength among the two parties at the state level.

The analysis of the role orientations of state party leaders does not confirm the widely held belief that there has been an increase in the proportion of amateur versus professional leaders within the party organizations and that this "new breed" of amateur leader is weakening the party organizations. Since 1960, there has been only a modest increase in the proportion of amateur state party leaders. The analysis did not reveal that either an amateur or a professional role orientation on the part of the state party chair has an impact on the structure and program of the state party.

The process of socializing state party chairs as they take on responsibility for an increasingly institutionalized party with a bureaucratized headquarters operation may account for the lack of relationship between chairperson role orientations and party organization attributes. This model is consistent with the findings of Maggiotto and Weber (1978) who studied the impact of county chair role orientations on county party organizations. They determined that an organizational imperative operates to cause even amateur activists to engage in activities that recognize common organizational needs of the local party. Given the greater structure and institutionalization of state party organizations, state chairs are likely to find organizational demands particularly compelling. A strong hunch, which builds on our analysis, is that amateurs and professionals alike have an instrumental regard for party organization, pursuing party office as a means to accomplishing ends which may be divergent, and, when in office, seeking to strengthen the party as a vehicle for pursuing those ends.

NOTES

1. These include Fortenberry's (1937) dissertation on "Legal Regulation of Political Party Organization in the United States," Starr's (1940) study of "The Legal Status of American Political Parties," and Berdahl's articles on "Party Membership in the United States" (1942). More recently, see National Municipal League (1965) on presidential nominating procedures, Childs' (1967) compilation of information on party organization, Huckshorn (1976) and Davis (1971) analyzing state law and party rules pertaining to the organization and processes of parties, Crotty's (1974) compendium of presidential nominating procedures in the states, the 1976 Chamber of Commerce of the United States' compilation of state and federal election campaign laws, and the four volume study by Robeck, Dyer and Woods (1978) on ballot access, for the Federal Election Commission's National Clearing House on Election Administration. Also see the extensive *Harvard Law Review* note on election law (1975). The emerging prominence of this field is suggested by the appearance in 1983 of a new *Journal of Law and Politics*, published at the University of Virginia.

8

Party Organizations and
Party Transformation

Robert Michels first posed the question "whether organizational forms of political parties [are] related in any significant way to the other characteristics of the party system or the polity in general" (Bernard Hennessy's paraphrasing, 1968, p. 5). In an era in which students of American parties are intensely concerned with the transformation of political parties and the party system, it is appropriate to pose the question next whether changes in the organizational forms of party are related in any significant way to the processes of party and system change. In this final chapter we attempt a partial synthesis of the findings presented earlier, as they relate to theories of party transformation.

The effort to understand change in parties and electoral systems is formally expressed in theories of party transformation.[1] If such a theory is to explain change in parties conceived in three-dimensional terms (party-in-the-electorate, party-in-government, and party-as-organization), it must specifically interrelate the three. The theory must permit us to respond to Michels' question and more. Broad-gauged theories of party transformation can only be tested by recourse to equivalently large and systematically collected data sets, covering the three dimensions of party and preferably allowing both longitudinal and cross-sectional analysis.[2] "Theories" that make a place for all three dimensions of party but are tested using only electoral data can do little more than tell us something about the dynamics of electoral change. This remains true despite occasional efforts to make generalizable inferences from the scattered data on party organizations or the role of party in government.

The abundance of reliable aggregate data on presidential, gubernatorial, and U.S. Senate and House elections (Robinson, 1934; Burnham, 1955; Scammon, 1956 et seqq.; David, 1972 et seqq.; Congressional Quarterly,

1975, 1977), and of survey data since 1952 on the attitudes and behavior of the presidential electorate (Center for Political Studies, University of Michigan; see, e.g., Campbell, Converse, Miller and Stokes, 1960; Miller, Miller and Schneider, 1980) satisfy the data needs for testing theories of electoral transformation. But a paucity of data on party organizations, and the limited data on party-in-government, have precluded testing hypotheses which relate these dimensions of party to the electoral dimensions.[3]

Efforts to compensate for this data lack have taken two principal forms. The first is the imaginative collating of continuous and nominal-level data as available to construct measures permitting rough comparison of organizational dimensions of party across the states (Weber, 1969; Olson, 1971). Useful as this effort has been, its inductive character and the practice of selecting from more than one dimension of party in assembling index measures of party organization, compounds at the conceptual level the "elusiveness" which has characterized party at the empirical level (Sorauf, 1975, pp. 40–41). It is not possible to test hypotheses on the impact of POS on RES, for example, if the measure of POS incorporates elements of electoral success.

The second mode of compensation for data limitations has been to define the problem away by making several key assumptions, including: (1) The assumption that the condition of party organization is a necessary consequence of changing levels of support for party in the electorate. Declining electoral support is assumed adequate basis for the inference that party organizations are in decline. (2) The functionalist assumption that the condition of party organization is a consequence of the extent to which the parties perform a stipulated repertory of "functions" or activities. Such functions include control over candidate recruitment, development and support in campaigns, and mobilization of the electorate (e.g., Key, 1956, pp. 11–12), as well as the responsibility to govern (Schattschneider, 1948, p. 23; APSA, 1950; Hardin, 1974). The substantial, although unsystematic, body of observation on these facets of party encourage scholars to make authoritative assessments of the condition of party organizations. (3) The assumption that the vitality of party organizations is determined by the values and expectations of elite activists (Kirkpatrick, 1976, p. 350), which is hinged to the further assumption that a "new breed" of "amateur" activists, embued with anti-organizational values, is permeating and threatening the existence of the party organizations (Wilson, 1962; Kirkpatrick, 1976). When linked together, these three bodies of assumptions, and the substantial, if fragmentary, data which they allow to be collated into a semblance of systematic knowledge, have greater persuasive power. But they are not adequate substitute for direct observation and testing of hypotheses which interrelate the three dimensions of party.

Party Organization Related to Other Dimensions of Party

By developing and operationalizing the concept of party organizational strength and by securing longitudinal and cross-sectional data permitting the scoring of party organizations on the strength variable, we have been able to test the hypothesis implicit in much of the writing on American parties, namely that as organizations they have been declining in strength since the 1950s. If, as V. O. Key asserted in 1956 (p. 287), most state parties were "virtually dead," our study demonstrates that the decades since have been a period of growth for party organizations at the local, state, and national levels. Party organizational change in a period of profound concern for the future of parties has been in the direction of strengthening the organizational attributes of individual party units, and the patterns of relationship among party units.

At the national level, the party organizations have experienced continuous development since the 1920s, despite electoral vicissitudes, in spite or because of longterm changes in the attitudes and behavior of the voting age population, and in the face of substantial enlargement of the regulatory and support roles of government in relation to parties and campaigns. Nor does this development seem to have been impeded by revolutionary change in the organizational environment of electoral politics (with, for example, the growth of political action committees from about 50 in 1970 to well over 3000 in 1984). Conceding that institutions may flourish up to the point of precipitous collapse and acknowledging what we consider to be the misguided assumption that changes in "function" or attrition of traditional functions necessarily erodes organizational strength, there is mounting evidence that the parties as organizations are being transformed toward an enlarged, rather than reduced, role in American politics. Through the "nationalization" of American parties, a process that has been recognized since the 1970s (Longley, 1978, 1980), national and state-local party committees have achieved levels of interdependence or "integration" in recent years which lack any historic parallel.

Figure 1.1 (Chapter 1) sketches the relationships relevant to determining the role of party organizations in the political system and in the processes of party and electoral change. Two broad categories of relationship are identified: those acting upon and determining the levels of party organizational strength, and those acted upon and influenced by the parties as organizations. Relative electoral success is depicted in the model as both contributing to party organizational strength and being affected by it. This reciprocal relationship is the subject of speculation in Chapter 5 where hypotheses are tested that relate   ES to POS independently and dependently. We are unable to confirm the impact of electoral success on party organizational strength. Hence we can offer no support for the prevalent tendency among political scientists to accept the strength of the party in the electorate as an indirect measure of the strength of party organizations. A second determinant of POS that is postulated in Figure 1.1 is public policy on parties. This reflects the view, prevalent in the discipline, that intrusive legislation has a weakening impact upon the parties. In cross-sectional analysis testing the contrary hypothesis that both support and regulatory legislation are associated with strong party organizations, we could detect no significant association of legislation on party and organizational strength (see Chapter 7). But we did find a weak relationship between supportive legislation and increases in organizational strength from the 1960s to the late 1970s, and a weak contrary trend for regulatory policy. Hence we conclude that the outpouring of legislation on parties and campaigning does not seem to have adversely affected the party organizations.

Aspects of the changing organizational environment of party are widely conjectured to have adverse consequences for parties as organizations. Two of these are the rise of amateurism, and of the role and influence of extra-party organizations. A "new breed" of activists are thought to have moved into organizational roles in swelling numbers bringing with them anti-organizational values which pose a threat to the future of party organizations. An exponential increase in the number of non-party political committees active in primary and general election campaigns is seen as an intrusion upon party turf and an obvious threat to the party organizations. Our data on state party chairs for the period 1960 to 1980 do not confirm the impression that the proportion of "amateurs" in party organizational leadership positions is increasing, nor do we find amateurism associated with weakening of attributes of party organizations. Our data on extra-party organizations afford basis for little more than informed speculation, but do suggest the possibility that party organizations are capable of adapting to and benefiting from the activities of such groups.

Traditionally, the hallmark of American party organization has been fragmentation. The state and local parties have been perceived as isolates that are only brought into the appearance of coherence fleetingly during the quadrennial presidential nominating season. For about a decade evidence has cumulated which suggests that in their different ways the two parties are being "nationalized"—that is, the state parties are being brought into interdependent relationship with the national parties, and in this process are becoming more aware of shared problems and opportunities across the states. Interviews with state party officials and surveys of former state party chairs undertaken as part of this study add to the stock of evidence on the nationalizing trend for the parties. Tests for the relationship between party integration (interdependence) and state party organizational strength yield results that suggest unexpected nuances in the relationship, but confirm the significance of elements of integration with the national party for the strength of state organizations of both parties.

However plausible, the assumption that the trend lines for parties as organizations will be closely parallel to those for electoral support of party, does not appear to merit confidence. The decade of the 1960s, which is generally recognized as a period of decline in popular support for party, witnessed what may have been a renaissance for state party organizations. More specifically, V. O. Key's expectation that increasing electoral competitiveness will have a revivifying impact on party organizations is not confirmed by our Chapter 5 analysis. On the other hand, the organizational strength of a party does appear to be related to increments in its share of the vote for governor. Through processes which we cannot pretend to explore, the congeries of bureaucratic and programmatic elements of the party organizational strength do make a difference in the vote. The strength of party organization does have an impact on the quality of the state party's relationship with officeholders, from the legislators to the governor.

Many of these relationships vary for the two major parties. While the conventional view has persisted that the parties were virtually extinct as organizations at the state and national levels in 1960, our measures of POS disclose that they were gaining in strength during the 1960s and, with a dip in the early 1970s, ended that decade significantly stronger than in 1960. But there are important party differences, and on the average, Democratic state parties are organizationally weak compared to the Republicans, and this is true for every section of the country. Over time, the electorally weaker party has shown the greatest organizational effort. In the sphere of national-state party integration, we confront dramatic contrasts in the styles of the two parties (the Democrats focusing on defining norms and enforcing compliance; the Republicans emphasizing service) but not in consequences. Despite the alternative emphases, both sets of state party chairs appear to take something from their relationship with the national party committees which contributes to state party organizational strength. Examining the impact of POS, we find pronounced party differences in linkage with officeholders. Republican POS is associated with high levels of linkage with both governors and legislators, while Democratic is associated with one or the other. We surmise that, within the bounds of POS associated with higher linkage, the relatively lower strength of Democratic organizations forces upon those state parties a choice between alternative emphases, while the Republicans can afford both.

Finally we must take note of the regional differences to be found within the parties. Table 2.8 (Chapter 2) shows changes in levels of party organizational strength by region and over time. The data suggest stability in the rank order of regions by mean level of Democratic state party organizational strength between the first (1960–1964) and fourth (1975–1980) periods studied: Midwest, West, Northeast, and South (but we are unable to score Northeast for the first period). The Republican pattern is not dissimilar except for the dramatic shift of the South from last to second position over the two periods. Varying patterns of change in mean level of state party strength regionally from the first to the fourth periods suggest patterns of party building for the two parties which could in some degree reflect perceptions of changing electoral strength and the need to compensate for changing patterns of competitiveness. Organization-building by one party, of course, can provide inducement to the other to invest in like activity. Thus we find the greatest activity for both parties in the South, where each registered its highest gains in strength. For the Republicans, this was followed by the Northeast, and more modestly, the Midwest and West. The Democrats register gains in the West and a net deficit for the Midwest. This suggests the existence of party strategies to use organizational resources to nudge electoral change one way or the other. But the relationship between organizational change and electoral change should be assessed.

In summary, our findings cast doubt on assumptions and on conventional understanding of the facts that have shaped thinking about American parties and theorizing about party transformation. Electoral support is not a reliable indicator of the condition of party organizations, which must be ascertained by direct observation guided by an adequate set of *a priori*-established conceptual subdimensions. So measured, the parties are found to have gained in organizational strength over a period when they were generally thought to be in decline. The strength of the state party organizations is associated with their relations with the national parties, as it is to electoral success, and linkage with officeholders. The Republicans, the electorally weaker party, seem to be organizationally stronger and it is that party that has shown the most substantial change in its pattern of regional strength from 1960–1964 to 1975–1980.

Some will think the increasing strength and integration of the party organizations to be associated with the process which Michels identified for the social democratic parties of Europe, where "from a means, organization becomes an end" (1962, pp. 190, 338). But the party organizations' preoccupation with organizational ends need not prevent them from influencing the political process and the course of electoral change. For it seems clear that however inward-looking state and national party committees may become, they will continue to include the exertion of electoral influence among their organizational goals.

The concluding part of this chapter focuses upon specific theories of party transformation or realignment and suggests within that framework of propositions, speculation, and data analysis, how inclusion of concern for party organization might influence the results.

Party Organization in a Theory of Party Transformation

A consensus has evolved on a developmental model permitting three alternative outcomes: (1) continuance of the present party system, (2) party realignment, possibly characterized by the entry of a new party and demise of one of the present major parties, or (3) an end to the party system and to the role of parties in the American polity. At best, the principal theorists of party transformation, Burnham, Sundquist, and Ladd and Hadley, are vague in their treatment of parties as organizations. Burnham (1970, p. 27) attributes critical realignment in large part to the unadaptive behavior of the party in government, as it fails to produce policy outputs responsive to the needs of new elements in a changing electorate. The condition of the party institutions, changing rules of the game, and transformation of modes of campaigning are for him subordinate themes to "the exceptionally rapid erosion of the behavioral hold of the old major parties on the American electorate" (p. 92), as he documents the decomposition of Amerian parties. Sundquist's (1973) etiology for realignment differs from Burnham's. Realignments are the consequence not so much of the performance of party in government and the shifting attachments of the electorate, but are triggered by the emergence of transcendent issues which cut across party lines and polarize the electorate. Although his model of the realignment process admits a role for the parties as organizations (pp. 275–98), he like Burnham, sees the traditional party organizations in "irreversible" decline (p. 352). Ladd and Hadley (1978, pp. 24–25), who deny the usefulness of the emphasis upon critical elections that is associated with realignment theory, concern themselves with the electoral impact of "the accumulation of social change" over time. At the very beginning of their analysis they differentiate the three dimensions of party and record their focus on electoral coalitions (p. 2, fn. 1).

By stipulating the weakness, indeed the decomposition, of party organizations, Burnham and Sundquist clearly imply a role for organization in their theories. The reiteration of decline of the party organizations further suggests that to demonstrate the absence of decline, or the strengthening of party organizations over recent decades, is tantamount to identifying a major anomaly in the theories. If party in the electorate is in process of erosion, and parties as organizations are stronger now than in the past, this conjunction of trends does not conform to the expectations derived from theories of party transformation. For in these theories, weakening of party ties in the electorate is consistently associated with the decline of party organization. The findings which have emerged in this study and which are summarized in the preceding section, require that we address afresh the issue of party transformation. We cannot undertake to revise the principal theories of party transformation which have guided scholarly expectations of the parties and party system in recent decades, but do attempt to indicate the significance of our work for such theories. The focal point of reference will be Burnham's work, since he has played the pivotal role in systematizing and generalizing Key's original notion of "critical elections."

Burnham's *Critical Elections and the Mainsprings of American Politics* (1970) is ambitious in sweep, apocalyptic in tone, startling in conclusions, and altogether one of the most important contributions to the literature of political science in his generation. From our vantage point the central strengths of the book are: (1) Burnham's measurement (the party discontinuity variable) which permits documentation of the periodicity of electoral realignments in American history; (2) his imaginative pursuit and analysis of a collage of data as a basis for conclusions about secular trends for all three dimensions of party; and (3) his specification of mechanisms whereby electorate, party organization, and party in government interact in the context of change.

Using aggregate data on voting for president, Burnham establishes "cutting points" at which "abrupt transformations" in popular voting patterns occur, such that the preceding majority/minority party relationships are reversed, or the components of the party system are changed. These disruptions, which occur about once each generation, have been preceded by periods of intense "erosion of the behavioral hold of the old major parties on the . . . electorate" or electoral disaggregation (1970, pp. 5, 92). Empirically, electoral disaggregation has in the past been prelude to mobilization, but it is not so linked in theory. Burnham thinks that the process of electoral disaggregation that can be traced to the mid-1960s "may point toward the progressive dissolution of the parties as action intermediaries in electoral choice and other relevant acts" (pp. 91–92, 130–31). That all three dimensions of party have experienced long term decline since about 1896, so that the periodic realignments have occurred against a backdrop of secular party "decomposition," is further suggestive of the impending dissolution of parties and the party system.

The "oscillation between the normal inertia of mass electoral politics and the ruptures of the normal which realignments bring about" may be explained in large part by the tendency of the majority party to continue to produce policy outputs suited to its founding coalition, and thus to be unresponsive to changing social and economic conditions and, especially, the changing composition of the electorate (pp. 27, 135–37):

It may well be that American political institutions, including the major political parties, are so organized that they have a chronic, cumulative tendency toward underproduction of other than currently 'normal' policy outputs. They may tend persistently to ignore, and hence not to aggregate, emergent political demand of a mass character until a boiling point of some kind is reached.

But that gap standing alone does not suffice to precipitate a realignment. Also needed is a "detonator . . . , some triggering event of scope and brutal force great enough to produce the mobilizations required from a normally passive-participant middle class electorate" (p. 170). Burnham sees these precipitants as "disasters" which "must not only be profound but must be in the nature of sharp, sudden blows;" and he has found that the "recurrent collapses of an unregulated market economy have, historically, been among the most important" such disasters (p. 171).

A transition from the old sytle "militarist" to the "mercantilist" approach to campaigning for presidential office is also credited with weakening the party nexus with the electorate (Burnham, pp. 78, 96, citing Jensen, 1968). The "militarist" campaign can be conducted in confidence by a party which is organized at the precinct level and can effectively mobilize the party allegiants in the electorate. Winning is a matter of reinforcement and logistics. The "mercantilist" type campaign is attractive to a candidate whose only realistic hope of winning is to cross party lines and appeal to the broad electorate. The effective manipulation of symbols and of advertising are counted upon to attract votes which represent defection from normal party identification. Woodrow Wilson's 1916 campaign is credited with the introduction of the mercantilist or advertising approach, which focuses attention on the candidate and has the purpose of blurring party lines. The spread of this approach after 1916 is deemed disastrous to the parties.

Within Burnham's model all three dimensions of party are in secular decline ("decomposition"). The failure of "party as an action intermediary" (pp. 177–78) and of party in government to respond to changing demands and changing conditions heightens the electorate's susceptibility to triggering events. Burnham is very much concerned with the state parties, even though his party discontinuity measure is derived from aggregate presidential votes. Until 1932, realignments occurred quickly and tended to affect all of the states simultaneously. However the "uneven" pace of the 1932 realignment across the states (Burnham, pp. 98–99; Sundquist, Ch. 11, speaks of "aftershocks") gives rise to the need to explain variance in terms of forces within the states.

While it is not possible to go back and establish strength measures for the state party organizations for the New Deal era, we have established a post-1950s pattern of bureaucratic and programmatic strength on the part of the state party organizations that suggests, at the least, reversal of what Burnham sees as a negative linear trend extending to the present. The structure of political parties appears to be in process of modernization and adaptation to a changing political environment, rather than "archaic and increasingly rudimentary" as depicted by Burnham (p. 181). This process of party organizational change, and especially the inordinate organizational effort of the minority Republican party, may be responsive to the processes of electoral change recorded by Burnham, and may indeed, be associated with an emerging style of politics in which the party organizations persist and relate to the electorate in ways different from the past.

We are in no position to challenge the thesis that the parties have failed as "action intermediaries." However, in addition to the integrative patterns documented within the parties (the relations, for example, of the national and state party organizations and the processes of "nationalization"), the parties do relate to officeholders, and the strength of the party organizations is relevant to such linkages. "Intermediary" denotes a middleman role as source of linkage between other actors, classically, between the public or electorate and government. The demonstrated significance of party organization for vote-winning, suggests the capacity of party organizations to influence electoral behavior. And, as the differential emphases of the two parties on organization building may suggest, the effort of the minority party to compensate for electoral weakness by attaining organizational strength, the regional variations within and between the parties may be part of the field of forces within the states which influence the uneven mark of realignment processes across the states.

All this is suppositious and tentative, as is appropriate in trying to come to grips with processes of party transformation. For all such efforts, however definitive and apocalyptic their tone, patterns are weaved out of hard and soft data, assumptions and perceptions, but the final product is in part testament to the imagination and insight of the author. Pursuing this speculative mode a bit further, we suggest that the United States since the turn of the century has experienced fundamental changes in the social system that have had a transforming impact upon electoral politics. This transformation has caught up with and engulfed the realignment cycle which Burnham documents. It is noteworthy that Burnham finds the 1932 realignment distinct from earlier such party shifts in the protracted period which was required after 1932 to give it national effect, and that in 1975 he concluded that the realigning process no longer sufficed to explain party change. In short, he seems to bring us back to Ladd and Hadley's emphasis upon social transformations which bring about changes in the composition, values, and demands of an electorate that when cumulated effects a "shift from one sociopolitical era to another" (p. 31) without regard to the intermediacy of parties.

We suggest that the rise of national party organizations in the 1920s and the rise or rebirth of state party organizations in the states in the decades following World War II are relevent to the realignment thesis. Burnham's use of Richard Jensen's (1968) distinction between militarist and mercantilist approaches to campaigning may provide a key to understanding the changing attributes and roles of party organizations as they relate to realignment.

The introduction of mercantilist-style campaigning in Wilson's 1916 campaign is very nearly coincidental with the rise of public relations on the American business scene, and only briefly precedes Wilson's introduction of public relations as a governmental function. It was George Creel, who had worked in the 1916 Democratic campaign, whom Wilson tapped to head the wartime Committee on Public Information (Kelley, 1956, p. 13 and n. 11; Creel, 1947; Bloom, 1973, pp. 8–17). Public relations was the core staff function in the national party committees as they were transformed from ephemeral election-year operations into full-scale organizations with permanent headquarters, specialized staff, budget, program, and eventually, fulltime leadership in the decades following World War I. Thus the public relations approach, which is associated with the differentiation of candidate campaigning from the traditional party organizations, is associated with the emergence of modern, bureaucratized party organizations.

Party leaders in the 1920s associated professionalized party organization with presidential election-winning. Democratic national party leaders associated organization with mobilizing a potentially Democratic but distressingly Republican electorate in the specific effort to bring about a realignment of the parties. After 1932, the Republican organizationalists argued this approach to saving the party from a prolonged role of subordination in presidential electoral politics.

The relationship between party organization and realignment at the state level can be illustrated by Wisconsin, which in 1948 became the last of the states to ratify the New Deal realignment (Burnham, pp. 24, 116–17). Wisconsin provides at the state level a rough parallel to the national Democratic party efforts to become more strongly organized during the 1920s. Wisconsin Democrats had been electorally dormant since the Civil War. In the twentieth century the politics of Wisconsin were at first fought between the stalwarts and the LaFollette progressives within the Republican party and after 1932 between the Republicans and the Progressives, which had splintered off. Senator Robert LaFollette, Jr. disbanded the Progressive party in 1946 and reentered the GOP, only to be defeated by Joseph McCarthy in the primary that year. With the Democratic National Committee keeping in touch, offering encouragement, and eventually, granting formal recognition in the form of the Call to the Democratic National Convention, a coalition of former Progressives, Milwaukee Socialists, disgruntled Democratic regulars, and returning young World War

II veterans set up an alternative to the moribund Democratic state central committee and launched a successful effort to turn the politics of the state around. Like the Democratic National Committee in the 1920s, they sought to use organization to accomplish, or perhaps more accurately for the Wisconsin Democrats, to consolidate a realignment (Haney, 1970).

On the basis of his study of electoral change from 1932 to 1970 in 18 formerly Republican states, Greenhalgh (1973, p. 320) gained the clear, although not fully documented, impression that the realignment "along Democratic lines in a number of the states had to await the emergence of a liberal, activist leadership clique . . . who wrested control of the state Democratic party from the conservatives in their states." We can only be speculative here, but for national and state party organizations we see strong roles in seeking to facilitate or to consolidate, to thwart or to minimize the consequences of a realignment, as suits the circumstances and the interests of the party. At the national level, the Democrats clearly perceived creation of an effective party organization as being a condition of survival in an electoral environment which then appeared intensely threatening.

The Republicans, in the first year of the New Deal, preached organization for the out party as the key to mitigating the adverse consequences of Democratic hegemony. In subsequent decades they practiced organization as a key to reversing electoral adversity. In short, the national party organizational elites in the 1920s and 1930s perceived a relationship between long-term electoral trends and organizational strength. In any formal way we cannot test for the accuracy of those perceptions, nor for the replication of these relationships at the state level. We can only seek to offer an alternative to the "orthodox suppositions" (Key, 1953, p. 525) of party organizational atrophy and the absence of organizational capacity to exert influence on the course of electoral system change.

The emergence of modern party organizations and the levels of strength of the party organizations at the national and state levels are necessary components of any effort to explain realignment processes. Although it is difficult to document the role of party organizations in realignment, the Democratic parties have become increasingly well organized and integrated under the spur of Republican organizational and electoral competition at the state level with incentives provided by the national Democratic party. The Republican state parties are accustomed to using organization in the attempt to compensate for their electoral disadvantage. The results of all this should be increasing electoral competition at the national and statewide levels; that is, the overall consequences should be counter-realigning. By necessary implication if the Burnham and Sundquist theses are to provide the framework for analysis, the party organizations of today must have some capability for doing two things. The first is to moderate the gap between government production of outputs and the changing demands of a changing electorate. And the second is to absorb the major transforming issues which appear on the political scene and to provide the axis for dividing the public on them. These, of course, are functions associated with the Burnham and Sundquist theories. The role that we perceive for parties, in stripping the "realignment" process of the quality of sudden disruption which Burnham associates with it, is perfectly consistent with Ladd and Hadley's understanding of the nature of political change in America.

An alternative scenario which fits party organization into the paradigm of party change might develop somewhat as follows: Parties are, as Burnham, Sundquist, and Ladd and Hadley speculate, vehicles for accommodating social change. A major way in which they serve this function is by accepting and socializing elite representatives of groups which have previously been politically passive, or excluded from politics, or new entrants by way of age or immigration. At the same time that the party organizations in their various manifestations provide an arena for competition of these new elites, and have a socializing impact upon them, the parties are changed by their participation. The new elites seek to change the party agendas to reflect their interests, needs and wants; the new elites seek representation among the party candidates for office and to benefit from the elite patronage which accrues to party organizational activity. Thus Ladd and Hadley reiterate the theme of "change within continuity" (p. 89), which in the context of this discussion would serve to point out that the party organizations are changed by and change the new elites. The processes of politics are, however, in their general outlines and forms, not radically different from the past. While the entry of these new elites into the traditional party organizations has been interpreted in terms of the infusion of new values which threaten the continued electoral efficacy of the parties (Ranney, 1975; Kirkpatrick, 1976), we find in Chapter 7 that when these attitudes are manifested in the form of the "amateur" and "professional" clusters (Wilson, 1962), they do not correlate with the expected anti-organizational consequences. As Michels wrote some seventy years ago, it is likely that "the struggle between the old leaders and the new" will result "not so much [in] a *circulation des elites* as a *reunion des elites*, an amalgam, that is to say, of the two elements" (1962 edition, p. 182).

Since the realignment of 1932, emerging groups have become increasingly important to the electoral success of the Democratic Party. For example, witness Jimmy Carter's victory in 1976 with the overwhelming majority of the black vote and a minority of the white vote both in the South and nationally. Such electorally important groups, however, do not necessarily hold party organizational power commensurate with their electoral contributions and the elite representatives of these emerging groups therefore seek power within party organizations. The Democrats have been struggling since the 1930s with the problem of bringing into the party management processes the elites of groups that have become critical to the party's electoral fortunes (Cotter and Bibby, 1980, pp. 19–25). Indeed, the Democratic reforms of the 1970s and 1980s are but a culmination of that process (Crotty, 1978; Polsby, 1983; and Price, 1984). In this period the Republican party has been influenced by the changes in state law which were a spinoff of the Democratic "reforms" but also has created party groups to make recommendations toward enlarging the role of women, minorities, and youth in the party. While the Democratic National Committee has more than doubled in size since 1974, with balanced representation of demographic and interest groups as part of the objective, the Republicans increased the *ex officio* voting membership of the RNC Executive Committee from 11 to 26 during the 1970s, creating positions for ethnic, black, and Hispanic representatives and doubling the number of positions slated for women and youth. As Austin Ranney puts it, "all conflict over party reform is, at bottom, conflict over who should be running the parties, and through them the nation" (1975, p. 144). The end result of a period of such conflict is likely to be that the new elites are secure in their access to positions of party influence, and the "regulars" will have held onto strategic influence in the party.

The party organizations influence the public agenda and act to transmit change in the ways that Burnham, Sundquist, and Ladd and Hadley suggest. Burnham's mechanism for change involves the underproduction by government of policy outputs responsive to the emergent groups in society and the consequent generation of demand which is channeled to intraparty and interparty competition. Sundquist sees the parties struggling to relate to "major realigning issues" which invariably concern the "appropriate objectives" of government and are perceived by the electorate in terms of "the composition and intrinsic nature of a *party*" (Sundquist, 1973, p. 279). As part of the metamorphosis, issue publics seek to influence party positions and nominations, intermediate to precipitating favorable electoral choices and preferred public policy change. Ladd and Hadley suggest that the party system will reflect "the social group composition and interest configurations" of society, and thus they tend to view change in evolutionary terms and they emphasize the possibilities for the expression of cumulatively large change within each of the parties without any necessary alteration of the general competitive relationship between them (pp. 90–91). In Chapter 2, we demonstrated the organizational capacity of the state parties to accommodate such social and political forces. And, in Chapter 6 we examined the capacity of the parties to establish linkage with elected policymakers. The necessarily limited scope of this study permits only the confident assertion that party organizational *capacity* exists which, at the state level, would make it possible for parties to react (presumably in self-protective ways) to the key forces for change in the transformation theories reviewed here.

While our focus is on the role of party organizations in the process of party transformation, as we turn to the relationship between the party organizations and the electorate it is necessary to question the assumption of a fractionating or hostile electorate which is indifferent to parties and politics. We leave it to others to address the soundness of the interpretations of attitudinal and electoral behavior data which lead to such a bleak depiction of American voters. The economic, social and technological forces which have contributed to reshaping the party organizations, the public agendas, and the electoral arena, must be expected to have left an impression upon the electorate. Norton Long (1962, p. 180) concluded that "the average man . . . has been taught to be a consumer of politics, a client rather than a self-directed principal." If the voter is not evidencing alienation, but rather an increasing degree of neutrality toward the parties (Wattenberg, 1981), it may not be fruitful to interpret party-electorate relations in terms of disaggregation and dealignment.

The inevitable tendency toward "good old days" analysis may lead us to not see or to misconstrue the adaptive behavior of contemporary party organizations which is very much in keeping with Easton's (1965, p. 84) stricture to the effect that system change is a condition of system persistence. Thus the success of party television, mass mail and tax checkoff appeals for funds suggest that the public is responsive to party use of modern communications technology. And the rule-of-thumb that mass mail appeals are more successful when accompanied by material placing the appeal within an issue or ideological context, further suggests the receptivity to such party-differentiating literature. The Republican National Committee has thrived on such appeals for two decades, and the Democratic National Committee is meeting with success as it moves to mass mailing solicitation. We find (Chapter 2) that the state party organizations are increasingly developing the capacity for utilizing mass communication techniques, while at the same time encouraging precinct-canvassing, registration, and get-out-the-vote activities by the local parties. This admittedly optimistic contribution to our scenario at least raises the possibility that the organizational strength of the parties can translate into influence with the electorate, albeit an electorate less prone by far than in the past to accept cues on the basis of the party symbol attached to them.

Adaptation of the parties to the separation of candidate campaigns from the party committees, development of funding capabilities, and of capacity on the part of the party organizations to exploit the "mercantilist" approach could combine to embue the party organizations with a counter-realigning, counter-dealigning capacity. The "nationalization" of the national and state parties might be interpreted as a further step toward achieving a concert of national and state organizational strength toward competing at the margins for the votes of a passively participant electorate. The parties have separated the level of party organizational strength from the level of electoral support and seek to influence a voter who is perceived to be a relatively neutral bystander.

For at least twenty years, political scientists and journalists have been conducting a death watch over the American parties, at first anticipating the extinction of one party system, and its replacement by another, but more recently heralding the imminent expiration of party as a force in American politics. Some of the more impatient watchers have gone so far as to conduct the obsequies without benefit of the corpse, others are seeking to apply resuscitatory techniques. The obsequies are undoubtedly premature, and the schemes for resuscitation may be guided by the effort to revive not so much the parties as the standard of "responsible party government."

It may well be that the changes observed in American party politics in the past few decades are changes which should be expected as a system of episodic voluntary associations gives way to modern institutionalized parties. The relationships of party organizational activists become less personal and occasionally more formal and routinized. Candidates freed by the primary from the vagaries of organizational leaders, and capable of hiring their own campaign technicians, become more separate from the party as organization and symbol. The electorate, whether moved by candidate or policy appeals, is more neutral toward the party symbols. And, the parties as organizations seek to deploy resources so as to render less threatening an environment teeming with competitive political groups, to make candidates and office-holders beholdened to the party organization, and to win votes in sufficient quantity, across enough states, and with sufficient regularity to retain the claim to participate in the dichotomization of that vote. This last resource involves meeting legal standards, traditionally set by the states and since 1972 by the federal government. This raises the last element in the agenda, namely that the parties are helped or hindered in their metamorphosis by public policy at the state and national levels which have rendered the parties into quasi-public entities, defined and embued with responsibilities by law.

It is arguable that not only has the emergence of the new breed of party had counter-realigning and especially counter-dealigning impact, but that, if Burnham is correct, we have moved beyond the stage of periodic realignments. If that is the case, the new phase is not one of partyless politics, but of the continuing party system composed of parties which operate within a framework of public regulation and support which protects more than weakens the existing parties.

NOTES

1. "Party transformation" is a conveniently inclusive term which subsumes both the dominant theory of party realignment in its alternative formulations (see, e.g., Burnham, 1970, Sundquist, 1973), and theories of party and electoral change which explicitly reject realignment as a major explanatory device (Ladd and Hadley, 1978). Transformation refers to fundamental processes of change which render parties and party systems distinguishable in character from their predecessors. Theories of party transformation may be middle-range or broad-gauged. A broad-gauged theory will, at the very least, attempt to explain the interaction of all three dimensions of party, party in the electorate, party organizations, and party in government in the context of change. A middle-range theory might deal with one or two of these dimensions, even while purporting to support generalizations encompassing all three. The most significant contributions to theories of party transformation are Key (1955, 1959), Burnham (1970), Sundquist (1973), Ladd and Hadley (1975), and Clubb, Flanigan and Zingale (1980). A growing literature is concerned with the special significance of processes of change for one party, with ramifying consequences for the party system (Phillips, 1969; Ladd, 1977a, 1977b; Burnham, 1982; Jones, 1984, forthcoming).

2. As early as 1948 Schattschneider (p. 25) cautioned that "the parties must be studied as a whole, at all levels of government, and in the electorate as well as in the government. To study national elections exclusively, as if a great substructure of state and local politics did not exist, is to invite misleading conclusions."

3. Until recently we have had no large body of systematically collected, comparative data on party organizations at the local, state and national levels to provide the basis for direct appraisal of the condition of the parties. In consequence, V. O. Key's 1956 assertion that most state parties were "virtually dead" (p. 287), which may have been accurate at that time, has been pressed into service to characterize the state parties in the succeeding decades. For the party in government, the research record is not quite so arid. And for the party in the electorate, the study of the presidential electorate and more recently, of congressional electorates, undertaken by the Center for Political Studies at the University of Michigan, has set standards which will be difficult to match.

As to the condition of party in government, the literature on congressional voting behavior has flourished since in 1951 when Julius Turner ended the long hiatus in such work. But there is a paucity of data on the relationship of the president to party (see Cronin, 1980; Cotter, 1983; Harmel, 1983; Ranney, 1983). At the state level, sporadic studies of legislative party cohesion (summarized in Jewell and Patterson, 1977) do not meet the data needs of a broad theory of party change. While the Center for Political Studies election studies have not been replicated at the state level (see Wright, 1974), numerous sources of reliable time series data and index measures are available that sustain generalizations about the electoral condition of parties in the states (see Burnham in CPS archives; David, 1972, et seqq.; Ranney, 1965, 1971, 1976; Bibby et al., 1983). Gubernatorial relations with the legislative parties, directed toward program enactment, has been the subject of substantial inquiry (see Morehouse, 1980, Chapter 5 for review of the literature), but has not produced data series suited to theory testing.

Appendix A

RESEARCH DESIGN—STATE PARTY ORGANIZATIONS

The Party Transformation Study involved the collection of data on party organizations at the national, state, and local levels. Data were collected for varying time periods between 1960 and 1980. This appendix provides details on the state-level portion of the project. (For details on the local-level portion of the study, see Appendix C.)

The most inclusive set of measures of party organizational strength concerns 54 state parties for the late 1970s. This sample of parties was selected by means of a systematic (non-random), stratified process. The objective in sampling was to maximize variation in the political environments and in the levels of strength of the state parties. Sampling strata were formed on the basis of four variables: (1) electoral success (see David, 1972 through 1978); (2) the power of the party in government (see Schlesinger, 1971); (3) public policy regarding primary, particularly, type of primary and nature of regulation (see Alexander, 1980); and (4) party institutionalization (see Weber, 1969). Sample states were selected so as to maximize representation of the strata defined by these variables. To the extent that discretion existed, states were selected to insure representativeness in terms of region, population, and percent of the population engaged in manufacturing. A series of t-tests confirmed that the sample states are not significantly different than non-sample states on the selection criteria (although the sample was not randomly selected). While these 54 state parties are not strictly a representative sample of the population of 100 state parties, they do reflect the entire range of variation on most variables commonly thought to influence the operation of parties. The states included in the sample, grouped by region, are: Northeast—Massachusetts, Connecticut, Rhode Island, New York, Vermont, West Virginia; South—Florida, Louisiana, Mississippi, Tennessee, Texas, Virginia, South Carolina; Midwest—Ohio, Michigan, Indiana, Illinois, Wisconsin, Iowa, Minnesota, Kansas; West—California, Colorado, Idaho, Oregon, Utah, Wyoming.[1]

In these 54 sample state parties, interviews with major party leaders provide the primary source of data on organizational attributes. Interviews were conducted with the state chairs of 53 of the 54 state parties; the executive directors of all 49 of the state parties employing an executive director; executive director "surrogates" in 4 of the 5 remaining states; two governors and a representative of the governor in 20 other states; and one national committee member each for 50 of the parties. For the purposes of the analysis of organizational strength, the data derived from interviews with the state chairs and executive directors are of greatest importance. A variety of data on party attributes was also collected during site visits to the party headquarters and from other archival sources.

Mailed questionnaires were used to collect similar information on the 46 non-sample state parties. Usable replies were receivable from 18 of the state chairs surveyed, for a response rate of 39 percent.

In order to be able to assess change over time the state chairs of all 100 state parties who served in the period 1960 to 1978 were also surveyed. After extended effort, a list of the addresses of the over 560 former state chairs was compiled and questionnaires were mailed. A response rate exceeding 61 percent was achieved through mail and telephone follow-ups.

Measurement Error

Two issues of measurement error are relevant to this research. First, we have relied on the party leaders to serve as informants to report on the attributes of their organizations. Social desirability may have led the leaders to over report the amount of activity and structure of their parties. There is no way of correcting for this although the problem is less severe for the data collected through personal interviews and site visits.

Second, we rely on recall data from the former state chairs of the party organizations. Recall data suffer from the inaccuracies of memories, and the problem is exacerbated in the reports of the chairs of the 1960s. We know of no way of corroborating the reports to correct for this bias. Unfortunately, we do not know what the effect of this bias is. A case can be made that faulty memory will tend to cause under reporting of activity and structure, but a case can also be made that it will lead to over reporting of activity and structure. However, sporadic, non-regularized activity is probably under reported for the earlier periods and properly reported for the later periods. Fortunately, this sort of activity is not part of what we consider to be organizational strength.

Sampling Error

We believe it possible to make some inferences about the nature of the (non-random) samples at each of the time periods. In the 1970s we have nearly complete data so our inferences from the samples to the population risk little error. This is not so for the 1960s; there the proportion of state parties represented in the data is low. However, it is quite plausible that our estimates of strength from the samples of the 1960s over estimate the population parameter. It is most likely that these samples are biased in favor of the relatively stronger parties. We suspect that the chairs of weaker party organizations were less likely to respond to the questionnaire because of the difficulty of doing so when, in effect, nearly all of the questions were irrelevant to them. We believe the response rate of the parties with skeletal organization and resources to be lower than the response rate of parties with substantial organization and resources. Consequently, our "base point," the early 1960s, provides a conservative standard against which change is assessed. This argument is speculative, of course, but nonetheless reasonable. (For empirical evidence on the effect of sampling error on the substantive conclusions, see footnote 3 in Chapter 2).

NOTES

1. The 23 non-sample states are grouped by region as follows: Northeast—Maine, New Hampshire, New Jersey, Delaware, Maryland, Pennsylvania; South—North Carolina, Georgia, Alabama, Arkansas; Midwest—Kentucky, Missouri, Oklahoma, Nebraska, South Dakota, North Dakota; West—Washington, Montana, Nevada, New Mexico, Arizona, Hawaii, Alaska.

Appendix B

EMPIRICAL DIMENSIONS OF STATE PARTY ORGANIZATIONAL STRENGTH

We have specified at the conceptual level the principal indicators of the concept "party organizational strength" and reported descriptive data on these attributes for state party organizations for the decades of the 1960s and 1970s. It is appropriate to consider whether these variables are equally useful measures of the concept, that is to determine how well they scale. The analytic technique employed for this purpose is factor analysis.

A factor analysis of the 12 principal indicators of party organizational strength for 289 state parties (i.e., 289 state chair respondents) from 1960 to 1980 produces results that are consistent with our expectations (Figure B.1). Three factors emerged in the unrotated solution (accounting for 33.2, 13.0, and 8.6 percent of the total variance, respectively). The lower half of Figure B.1 reports the pattern loadings resulting from biquartimin rotation.[1] The three factors are moderately-to-strongly intercorrelated and the factor structure is remarkably consistent with the *a priori* classification of items. The first factor clearly represents the programmatic capacity of state party organization. Three of the four institutional support program variables load on this factor, and the fourth variable, issue leadership, loads strongly on no factor. The two strongest loadings are for variables representing the candidate-directed activity and organizational complexity subdimensions, a finding inconsistent with the *a priori* placement of variables. Upon reflection, however, the inconsistency is easily resolved. Candidate service activity is indicated by whether the party organization conducts campaign seminars and whether it employs a field staff. Like institutional support activities, such programs reflect an enduring organizational capacity. The number of staff divisions is similarly interpretable: i.e. staff specialization is functionally related to the amount and type of activity of the party organization. Only the modest loading of the headquarters accessibility variable detracts from the interpretation that this first factor indicates institutional support activity.

Factor 2 is almost exclusively a measure of breadth of candidate recruitment activity. Although recruitment activity is related to money contributions to candidates ($r = .37$), the contribution variable has only a modest relationship to the factor. The other candidate-directed measures are even more weakly related to the factor. The domination of this factor by the

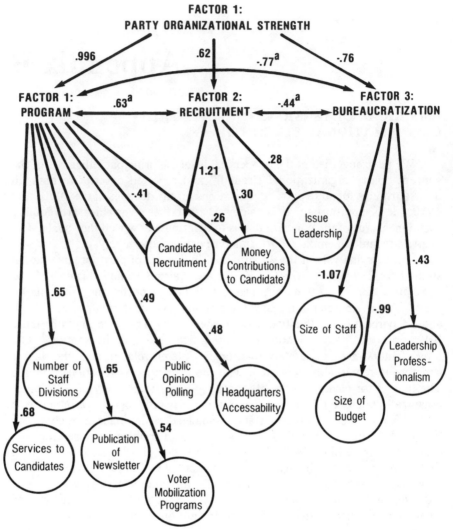

^{a} Correlation coefficients. Other coefficients are pattern loadings. All coefficients $\geq \pm .25$ are shown.
N = 289

FIGURE B.1. Interrelationships of State Party Organizational Strength Indicators and Factors.

TABLE B.1.
Indicators of State Party Organizational Strength.

Indicator	Correlations with Organization Strength Factor Score[a]
Number of Staff Divisions	.86
Services to Candidates	.78
Leadership Professionalism	.59
Voter Mobilization Programs	.58
Public Opinion Polling	.57
Size of Budget	.54
Size of Staff	.54
Publication of a Newsletter	.53
Money Contributions to Candidates	.45
Headquarters Accessibilty	.45
Candidate Recruitment	.36
Issue Leadership	.22

[a]$N = 289$.

breadth of recruitment indicator is perhaps a function of the nature of the recruitment activity variable (see p. 175). In any event, there is only weak support for the expectation that the four variables are valid indicators of candidate-directed activity.

Three of the four organizational complexity measures have strong loadings on the third factor. The factor is most strongly defined by the budget and staff variables, with a relatively modest loading of the leadership professionalism indicator. The accessibility of the party headquarters does not appear to be a significant indicator of complexity, perhaps because so many organizations satisfy this minimal requirement of bureaucratization.

Generally, the data comport fairly well with our expectations. Three factors were expected from the factor analysis and three emerged. However, the factors are not as "clean" as might be hoped (although they rarely are in factor analysis) and the derived factors are themselves strongly inter-correlated. These correlations are expected in that all of the variables are indicators of a common concept—party organizational strength. Although organizational complexity and programmatic capacity may be conceptually distinct, it was never expected that their measures would be empirically unrelated.[1] Consequently, a higher order factor analysis was performed on the three factor scores. As shown in the upper half of Figure B.1, each of the three components loads strongly on the factor with the program component having the strongest relationship. Obviously, only a single factor emerged (accounting for 75 percent of the observed variance) so no rotation was performed. This summary measure of party organizational strength is still strongly related to the original indicators. Table B.1 reports the bivariate correlations of the strength factor score and each of the twelve measures. There is certainly variation in the strength of the correlations, but it was never assumed or expected that the variables were equally useful indicators of the concept. The strong correlation of number of staff divisions and organizational strength reflects the dual function of this variable (i.e., it serves as a measure of complexity and of program) and the very weak correlation of issue leadership and strength reflects the greater service orientation of party programs. Thus, while there are components to the concept of "party organizational strength," it is not unreasonable to consider it unidimensional and to focus analysis on the summary measure.

NOTES

1. Typically, orthogonal rotation is used in factor analysis. We rejected this approach as inappropriate because we posit no theoretical expectation that the various dimensions of party organizational strength are unrelated to each other. For instance, we do not believe that structure and activity are unrelated. To use orthogonal rotation would be to force a structure on the data that we believe is substantively inappropriate.

Appendix C

RESEARCH DESIGN—LOCAL PARTY ORGANIZATIONS

In order to characterize the attributes of local party organizations, a survey of substate party leaders was undertaken. In most of the states, leaders of the county party organization were surveyed. In the following states, leaders of county-equivalent "noncounty" party units were surveyed: Connecticut, Massachusetts, and Rhode Island (towns); Alaska and North Dakota (districts); Minnesota (districts and/or counties); Louisiana (for Democrats, parishes; for Republicans, parishes and Political Action Council Districts); New Hampshire, (Republicans only, towns and counties); and Virginia (cities and counties). Miscellaneous other aberrations in organization (e.g., St. Louis City in Missouri) were also accommodated. Although we received a few responses from congressional district chairs (from persons who were included in the sample because of their former role as county chairs), these responses have been omitted. Thus, the analysis is of county or county-equivalent party units. To simplify matters, these units will be referred to as "local party organizations."

Over 7300 questionnaires were mailed to these local party leaders. The mailings began in 1979 and extended through 1980. Non-responding leaders received up to three waves of mailings, each including a copy of the questionnaire. If they still failed to respond, they were sent an abridged, much shortened form of the questionnaire. A final, fifth effort was made to secure a response from states in which the response rate was below average and from major counties in each of the states (defined in footnote 5, Chapter 3). Because of the importance of these major counties, their leaders were also telephoned to encourage completion of the questionnaire. As a result of these efforts, over 4000 questionnaires were received.

Some ambiguity exists in calculating the response rate to the survey. Approximately 7300 subjects were included on the lists of chairs and responses were received from roughly 4000 of these. However, in some states (e.g., Kentucky, Ohio, and Minnesota) the Republicans routinely have co-chairs, and there are sporadic instances of co-chairs in all states for both Republicans and Democrats. After reducing the accepted responses to one per county party by eliminating the response of one of the co-chairs, 3746 county-equivalent party organizations were represented. Twelve of these were discarded because the state in which the organization was located could

TABLE C.1.
Response Rates of County Chairs.

State	Number of Counties	Democrats			Republicans		
		Number Mailed	Unorganized	Counties Represented	Number Mailed	Unorganized	Counties Represented
Alabama	67	67	0	34	61	6	21
Alaska (Districts)	22	4	0	2	19	5	6
Arizona	14	14	0	11	14	0	6
Arkansas	75	74	1	29	71	2	24
California	58	53	5	30	56	1	28
Colorado	63	62	4	45	63	1	40
Connecticut (towns)	169	169	0	92	168	0	73
Delaware	3	3	0	1	3	0	3
Florida	67	67	0	33	45	21	27
Georgia	159	159	1	58	88	70	31
Hawaii	4	4	0	3	4	0	1
Idaho	44	43	1	21	44	0	29
Illinois	102	101	0	43	190	0	65
Indiana	92	92	0	58	91	1	49
Iowa	99	100	0	68	99	0	66
Kansas	105	84	19	51	99	6	54
Kentucky	120	118	2	67	167	25	53
Louisiana (parishes)	64	62	0	17	59	15	21
Maine	16	15	0	11	17	0	9
Maryland	24	25	0	12	23	0	11
Massachusetts (towns)	351	315	0	160	299	0	115

Michigan	83	83	1	37	81	0	42
Minnesota	87	79	8	52	166	4	61
Mississippi	82	88	0	27	82	1	41
Missouri (+1 City)	115	114	0	74	112	3	56
Montana	57	52	4	37	52	4	22
Nebraska	93	75	18	46	91	2	42
Nevada	17	17	0	7	17	0	7
New Hampshire	10	10	0	7	14	0	4
New Jersey	21	20	0	11	21	0	9
New Mexico	32	32	0	12	32	0	19
New York	62	62	0	37	62	0	36
North Carolina	100	100	0	54	96	2	43
North Dakota	53	49	0	30	48	0	17
Ohio	88	89	0	57	190	0	75
Oklahoma	77	78	0	45	140	3	45
Oregon	36	34	1	19	36	0	17
Pennsylvania	67	65	1	30	67	0	38
Rhode Island (towns)	39	39	0	20	39	0	16
South Carolina	46	46	0	32	43	3	20
South Dakota	67	62	2	36	63	1	36
Tennessee	95	95	0	48	94	0	40
Texas	254	249	4	129	237	15	115
Utah	29	29	0	14	25	4	13
Vermont	14	14	0	12	13	1	7
Virginia	136	136	1	70	128	6	72
Washington	39	39	0	28	39	6	22
West Virginia	55	54	0	27	53	1	22
Wisconsin	72	70	0	42	72	0	44
Wyoming	23	24	0	14	22	0	9

not be identified. Of the 7334 (3667 × 2) such units in the U.S., at least 255 had no chair at the time of the survey (see below). Thus, in one sense, the response rate for organized party units can be considered to be 52.7 percent (3734 of the 7079 organized parties), and 100 percent for the unorganized units. The response rate for the major counties exceeds two-thirds.

While somewhat above average for research of this sort, the response rate poses substantial obstacles to estimating the attributes of substate party organizations. Most worrisome is that the sample of respondents may be biased in favor of more developed party organizations. It is likely that the non-respondents are disproportionately drawn from skeletal party organizations with weak leadership. While there is little way in which this bias can be compensated, at least one effort was made to adjust the data. When the lists of local party leaders provided by the state party organizations showed no local party chair, it was assumed that the party was "unorganized" in that county. For Democrats, 62 counties were identified as "unorganized;" for Republicans the figure was 193. Of course, these counties may not actually be unorganized, they may simply be in transition between chairs, although we believe that most of them are unorganized. Nevertheless, a completed questionnaire, reflecting no local party organization or activity, was added to the data for each unorganized county. These data no doubt underestimate the level of activity and structure of these organizations, but serve to compensate in some small degree for opposite bias among the responding counties.

In using the chairs as informants on the activity and structure of the local party organizations, a non-negligible amount of measurement error is no doubt introduced. It is apparent from some of our data (e.g., the responses of co-chairs) that the chairs do not always report information accurately. Several spurious variables may affect the reliability of the responses, e.g., proximity of the time at which the questionnaire was completed to an election period, and it is even likely that the responses of more highly developed organizations are more reliable than the responses of those organizations with sporadic activity, little formal structure, and little record keeping. Thus, our data may underestimate the level of development of these organizations.

It should be reiterated that the unit of analysis in this research is the organization, not the chair (although for other purposes it is appropriate to consider the responding individual as the unit of analysis). Of course, in a large majority of the states there is no difference between the two units. Thus, this is an analysis of a sample of 3989 county and county-equivalent party organizations. The basic attributes of the chairs and their organizations are shown in Tables 3.1 and 3.2 of Chapter 3. Details on response rates by state are given in Table C.1.

Appendix D

DIMENSIONS OF LOCAL PARTY ORGANIZATIONAL STRENGTH

While descriptive data on several indicators of the strength of local party organizations have been reported, it must be determined whether each of these variables is a suitable measure of the concept of party organizational strength. Furthermore, the basic dimensionality of party organizational strength has not been established at this point. We now turn to the development of a scale of organizational strength, including analysis of the factors associated with strong local party organizations.

From the various measures of local party program and structure that have been reviewed, several simple indices can be constructed. For organizational structure, these indices represent the degree to which the party organization has achieved the attributes roughly associated with levels of organizational development. Specifically, the attributes and measures are:

1. Ability to fill key leadership positions: a. whether the county level organization has a complete set of officers; and b. whether at least 90 percent of the precinct chair positions are filled. Most party organizations satisfy at least one of these requirements of bureaucratization (Democrats, 92 percent; Republicans, 82 percent).
2. Election-period organizational maintenance: a. whether the chair devotes at least six hours per week to party business during election periods; and b. whether the county-level committee meets at least bimonthly during election periods (Democrats, 83 percent; Republicans, 78 percent).
3. Formalization of structure: a. whether the local party organization has a constitution, rules, or bylaws; and b. whether it has a formal annual budget (Democrats, 71 percent with at least one; Republicans, 69 percent).
4. Non-election period organization maintenance: a. whether the chair devotes at least six hours per week to party business during non-election periods; and b. whether the county-level committee meets at

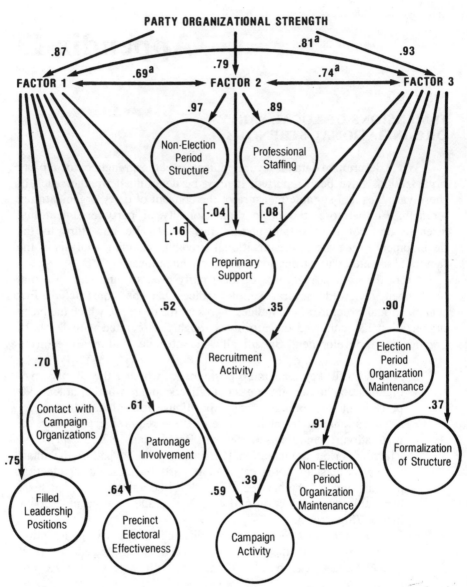

aCorrelation coefficients. Other coefficients are pattern loadings. All coefficients ≥ ± .35 are shown.
2455 ≤ N ≤ 3977

FIGURE D.1. Interrelationships of Local Party Organizational Strength Indicators and Factors.

least bimonthly during non-election periods (Democrats, 53 percent with at least one; Republicans, 54 percent).

5. Continuity of structure in non-election periods: a. whether the party organization has its own telephone listing; and b. whether the party maintains a year-round headquarters (Democrats, 18 percent with at least one; Republicans, 15 percent).

6. Professional staffing: a. whether the party organization has any paid (full- or part-time) staff; and b. whether the county-level chair receives a salary (Democrats, 9 percent with at least one; Republicans, 8 percent).

Thus, each party organization was awarded a score on each of six, two-item indices.[1]

In a similar vein, measures of the level of programmatic activity of the local party organizations were derived. Six multi-item indices were created:

1. Levels of contact and coordination with candidate campaign organizations.
2. Levels of candidate recruitment activity.
3. Levels of campaign activity.
4. Levels of involvement in patronage.
5. Electoral effectiveness of precinct-level organizations.
6. Pre-primary endorsements.

Each of these indicators was constructed from a variable number of items (between 1 and 12).

In order to consider their dimensionality, these twelve indicators of party structure and program were subjected to Common Factor Analysis. The factor solution, with oblique, biquartimin rotation,[2] is reported in Figure D.1. Because the results from separately analyzing Democratic and Republican organizations are virtually identical, Figure D.1 reports the factor structure resulting from the analysis of all of the county-level organizations combined.

The factor analysis results are consistent with our *a priori* treatment of each of the variables. The first factor represents organizational program and activity. The factor is strongly and nearly equally influenced by the activity indicators. The only exception is pre-primary support, acceptably related to none of the factors. Of course, pre-primary support is not a widespread practice and at least some chairs believe that the practice is dysfunctional to the development of the broad candidate constituency necessary to a strong party organization. Perhaps the only surprising component of this first factor is the strong loading of the leadership positions variable. Recalling that this is a measure of whether the county-level officer positions and the precinct-level chair positions are filled, this finding leads to the conclusion that in volunteer organizations, filled positions are a better indicator of the capacity for programmatic activity than of bureaucratization. Factor scores for this first dimension will be used to indicate levels of programmatic activity.

Factors 2 and 3 indicate party structure. The first of these represents organizations that function year round. Parties receiving a high score on this factor are those with professional, non-seasonal staffing and that operate a non-seasonal, year round party headquarters. In contrast, factor 3 concerns electoral period organization. The strong loading of non-election period organizational maintenance on this factor is no doubt an ipsative influence and thus does not detract from the interpretation of the factor. The modest loadings of the two activity variables is attributable to the degree to which these activities, in contrast to the others, require organizational structure to be performed.[3]

Three factors emerged from the factor analysis, and they are strongly interrelated. Parties engaging in substantial programmatic activity tend to be more highly structured. Parties with a year round operation tend also to have a structured organization during election periods. Indeed, these correlations are so substantial that they suggest the utility of treating party organizational strength as a unidimensional concept, with discernably related facets. Furthermore, the findings point to the usefulness of a second-order factor analysis. Such an analysis reveals a single factor, accounting for 83 percent of the variance in the three-factor correlation matrix. The loadings of the three subdimensions are: election period structure, (.86); programmatic activity, (.76); and non-election period activity, (.63). Factor scores from this second-order factor analysis will serve as a summary indicator of the organizational strength of the local party organizations.

Thus, the analysis reveals that the indicators of the organizational strength of local parties are unidimensional, a finding that closely parallels our conclusions about the organizational strength of state party organizations. By itself, this finding does not mean that local party organizations are highly bureaucratized, nor that they engage in substantial activity. Rather, where there is activity, there tends to be structure, and vice versa. Since it is useful to think of party organizational strength as a unidimensional concept, our analysis of its correlates need only rely on the summary second-order factor score.

NOTES

1. A seventh measure (continuity of the local party organization) was considered on the basis of data on the number of people holding the chair position since

1969 and whether the party organization had gone out of existence at any time in the preceeding ten years. This variable was so weakly (and in a few instances, negatively) related to the other indicators that it was dropped from further consideration.

In terms of the final summary index of party organizational strength, local parties with greater turnover in the chair position are significantly stronger. But conceptually and empirically, tenure stability contributes to strong state party organizations. This apparent contradiction may be caused by a curvilinear relationship; very low tenure stability and very high tenure stability may be associated with weak party organizations.

2. Oblique rotation was employed because we know of no theoretical reasoning which would lead to the expectation that the dimensions of party organizational strength are independent of each other (the assumption behind the more common orthogonal rotation).

3. Because we anticipate that the acquisition of structural attributes is a sequential, incremental process, the most appropriate scaling technique is actually Guttman Scaling. When the six indicators of organizational structure are dichotomized and subjected to Guttman Scaling, an acceptable scale is formed for the Republicans (coefficient of scalability = .652) and a nearly-acceptable scale is formed for the Democrats (coefficient of scalability = .581). This is a fairly impressive finding in that errors were counted using the unreasonably-demanding Goodenough technique (with SPSS). Because we sought to analyze data on structure and activity simultaneously, and because the dichotomization required by Guttman Scaling is wasteful of information, we have chosen to use factor analysis as the main scaling technique.

References

Alexander, Herbert E. (1980) *Financing Politics: Money, Elections and Political Reform*, 2nd Edition, Washington, D.C.: Congressional Quarterly Press.

_____, and Jennifer W. Frutig, editors (1982) *Public Financing of State Elections: A Data Book and Election Guide to Public Funding of Political Parties and Candidates in Seventeen States*, Los Angeles: Citizens' Research Foundation, University of Southern California.

American Political Science Association (APSA) (1950) *Toward a More Responsible Two-Party System*, New York, Rinehart.

Beck, Paul A. (1974) "Environment and Party: The Impact of Political and Demographic County Characteristics on Party Behavior," *American Political Science Review* (December), pp. 1229–44.

Berdahl, Clarence A. (1942) "Party Membership in the United States," *American Political Science Review* (February and April), pp. 16–50, and 241–62.

Beyle, Thad L. (1983) "Governors," Chapter 6 in Virginia Gray, Herbert Jacob, and Kenneth N. Vines, editors, *Politics in the American States*, Fourth edition, Boston: Little, Brown.

_____ and J. Oliver Williams, editors (1972) *The American Governor in Behavioral Perspective*, New York: Harper & Row.

Bibby, John F. (1979) "Political Parties and Federalism: The Republican National Committee," *Publius* (Winter), pp. 229–36.

_____ (1981) "Party Renewal in the National Republican Party," pp. 102–15 in Gerald Pomper, editor, *Party Renewal in America*, New York: Praeger.

_____, Cornelius P. Cotter, James L. Gibson, and Robert J. Huckshorn (1983) "Parties in State Politics," Chapter 3 in Virginia Gray, Herbert Jacob and Kenneth N. Vines, editors, *Politics in the American States*, Fourth edition. Boston: Little, Brown.

Black, Gordon S. (1975) "A Rational Choice Analysis of Alternative Party Scenarios," American Political Science Association paper.

Bloom, Melvyn H. (1973) *Public Relations and Presidental Campaigns*, New York: Crowell.

Burnham, Walter Dean (1955) *Presidential Ballots, 1836–1892*, Baltimore: Johns Hopkins Press.

—— (1970) *Critical Elections and the Mainsprings of American Politics*, New York: Norton.

—— (1975) "American Politics in the 1970's: Beyond Party?" pp. 308–57 in William Nisbet Chambers and Walter Dean Burnham, editors, *The American Party Systems: Stages of Development*, New York: Oxford.

—— (1976) "Revitalization and Decay: Looking Toward the Third Century of American Electoral Politics," *Journal of Politics*, (August), pp. 146–72.

—— (1982) "The Eclipse of the Democratic Party," *Democracy*, (July), pp. 7–17.

Campbell, Angus, Gerald Gurin, and Warren E. Miller (1954) *The Voter Decides*, Evanston: Row, Peterson.

——, Philip E. Converse, Warren E. Miller, and Donald E. Stokes (1960) *The American Voter*, New York: Wiley.

Chamber of Commerce of the United States (1976) *Campaign Finance: Analyses of State and Federal Election Campaign Laws*, (2 loose leaf vols.), Washington, D.C.

Childs, Richard S. (1967) *State Party Structures and Procedures: A State-by-State Compendium*, New York: National Municipal League.

Clubb, Jerome M., William H. Flanigan, and Nancy H. Zingale (1980) *Partisan Realignment: Voters, Parties and Government in American History*, Beverly Hills: Sage Publications.

Congressional Quarterly (1975) *Guide to U.S. Elections*, Washington, D.C. *Supplement*, 1977.

Conway, Margaret M. (1981) "Political Party Nationalization: Campaign Activities and Local Party Development." Midwest Political Science Association Paper.

Costikyan, Edward N. (1966) *Behind Closed Doors: Politics in the Public Interest*, New York: Harcourt, Brace & World.

Cotter, Cornelius P. (1983) "Eisenhower as Party Leader," *Political Science Quarterly* (Summer), pp. 255–83.

—— and Bernard C. Hennessy (1964) *Politics Without Power*, New York: Atherton Press.

—— and John F. Bibby (1980) "Institutional Development of Parties and the Thesis of Party Decline," *Political Science Quarterly* (Spring), pp. 1–27.

Creel, George (1947) *Rebel at Large*, New York: Putnam's.

Cronin, Thomas E. (1980) "The Presidency and the Parties," Chapter 11 in Gerald M. Pomper, editor, *Party Renewal in America*, New York: Praeger.

Crotty, William J. (1974) *Presidential Nominating Procedures: A Compendium of Election Practices in 1972*, (2 Vols.), New York: National Municipal League.

—— (1978) *Decision for the Democrats*, Baltimore: Johns Hopkins Press.

David, Paul T. (1972) *Party Strength in the United States, 1872–1970*, Charlottesville, Va.: University Press of Virginia.

—— (1974) "Party Strength in the United States: Changes in 1972," *Journal of Politics*, (August), pp. 785–96.

_____ (1976) "Party Strength in the United Staes: Changes in 1974," *Journal of Politics*, (May), pp. 416–25.

_____ (1978) "Party Strength in the United States: Changes in 1976," *Journal of Politics*, (August), pp. 770–80.

_____, Malcolm Moos, and Ralph M. Goldman, editors (1954) *Presidential Nominating Politics in 1952*, (5 Vols.), Baltimore: Johns Hopkins Press.

Davis, David M. (1971) *Legal Powers of State Chairmen: A Content Analysis of Party By-Laws and State Election Laws*, M.A. Thesis. Boca Raton: Florida Atlantic University.

Downs, Anthony (1957) *An Economic Theory of Democracy*, New York: Harper.

Duverger, Maurice (1954) *Political Parties*, New York: Wiley.

Dye, Thomas R. (1969) *Politics in States and Communities*, Englewood Cliffs, N.J.: Prentice-Hall.

Easton, David (1965) *A Systems Analysis of Political Life*, New York: Wiley.

Eckstein, Harry (1968) "Party Systems," *International Encyclopedia of the Social Sciences*, Vol. 11, pp. 436–53. New York: Macmillan/Free Press.

Eldersveld, Samuel J. (1964) *Political Parties: A Behavioral Analysis*, Chicago: Rand McNally.

_____ (1982) *Political Parties in American Society*, New York: Basic Books.

Epstein, Leon D. (1980) *Political Parties in Western Democracies*, New Brunswick, N.J.: Transaction Books.

Fenton, John H. (1957) *Politics in the Border States*, New Orleans: Hauser Press.

_____ (1966) *Midwest Politics*, New York: Holt, Rinehart and Winston.

Fortenberry, Charles N. (1937) *Legal Regulation of Political Party Organization in the United Staes*, Urbana: University of Illinois. Unpublished Ph.D. dissertation.

Francis, Wayne L. (1968) *Legislative Issues in the Fifty States*, Chicago: Rand McNally.

Gibson, James L., Cornelius P. Cotter, John F. Bibby, and Robert J. Huckshorn (1983) "Assessing Party Organizational Strength," *American Journal of Political Science*, (May), pp. 193–222.

Gray, Virginia, Herbert Jacob, and Kenneth N. Vines, editors (1983) *Politics in the American States*, Fourth edition, Boston: Little, Brown.

Greenhalgh, Gary L. (1973) *Emergence of Political Competition in Former One-Party Republican States*, Charlottesville, Va.: University of Virginia. Unpublished Ph.D. dissertation.

Gross, Donald A. (1981) "Changing Patterns of Interparty Competition: Presidential, Senatorial, House, and Gubernatorial Elections 1824–1978," Midwest Political Science Association Paper.

Haney, Richard Carlton (1970) *A History of the Democratic Party of Wisconsin Since World War Two*, Madison, University of Wisconsin. Unpublished Ph.D. dissertation.

Hardin, Charles M. (1974) *Presidential Power and Accountability*, Chicago: University of Chicago Press.

Harmel, Robert, editor (1983) *The President as Party Leader*, New York: Praeger.

———— and Kenneth Janda (1982) *Parties and Their Environments: Limits to Reform?*, New York: Longman.

Havard, William C., editor (1972) *The Changing Politics of the South*, Baton Rouge: Louisiana State University Press.

Harvard Law Review Note (1975) "Developments in the Law—Elections," (April), pp. 1111–339.

Hawley, Willis D. (1973) *Nonpartisan Elections and the Case for Party Politics*, New York: Wiley.

Heard, Alexander (1960) *The Costs of Democracy*, Chapel Hill: University of North Carolina Press.

Hennessy, Bernard C. (1968) "On the Study of Party Organization," pp. 1–44 in William J. Crotty, editor, *Approaches to the Study of Party Organization*, Boston: Allyn and Bacon.

Hofstetter, C. Richard (1973) "Organizational Activists: The Bases of Participation in Amateur and Professional Groups," *American Politics Quarterly*, (April), pp. 244–76.

Horn, Robert A. (1956) *Groups and the Constitution*, Stanford, Calif.: Stanford University Press.

Huckshorn, Robert J. (1976) *Party Leadership in the States*, Amherst: University of Massachusetts Press.

————, Cornelius P. Cotter, John F. Bibby and James L. Gibson (1982a) *The Social Background and Career Patterns of State Party Leaders*, (unpublished manuscript).

————, James L. Gibson, Cornelius P. Cotter, and John F. Bibby (1982b), "On the Resistance of State Party Organizations to Dealignment: National Parties as Agents of State Party Development," Iowa City: Shambaugh Conference Paper.

Jackson, John S. III, and Robert A. Hitlin (1981) "The Nationalization of the Democratic Party," *Western Political Quartlery*, (June), pp. 270–86.

Jacob, Herbert, and Kenneth N. Vines, editors (1965, 1971, 1976) *Politics in the American States*, 1st, 2nd, and 3rd Editions. Boston: Little, Brown. (For 4th Edition, see Gray, et al. 1983).

James, Judson L. (1974) *American Political Parties in Transition*, New York: Harper.

Jensen, Richard (1968) "American Election Campaigns: A Theoretical and Historical Typology." Midwest Political Science Association Paper.

Jewell, Malcolm E. (1967) *Legislative Representation in the Contemporary South*, Durham: Duke University Press.

———— (1982) *Representation in State Legislatures*, Lexington: University of Kentucky Press.

———— (1983) "The Impact of State Political Parties on the Nominating Process." Meeting of Midwest Political Science Association Paper.

———— and David M. Olson (1982) *American State Political Parties and Elections*, (Revised Edition), Homewood, Ill.: Dorsey Press.

_____ and Samuel C. Patterson (1977) *The Legislative Process in the United States*, (3rd Edition), New York: Random House.

Jones, Charles O. (1984, forthcoming) "Our Minority Party Politics: The Republican Challenge," *Society*.

Jones, Ruth S. (1980) "State Public Financing and the State Parties." pp. 283–303 in Michael J. Malbin, editor, *Parties, Interest Groups, and Campaign Finance Laws*, Washington, D.C.: American Enterprise Institute.

_____ (1981) "State Public Campaign Finance: Implications for Partisan Politics," *American Journal of Political Science*, (May), pp. 342–61.

Kelley, Stanley, Jr. (1956) *Professional Public Relations and Political Power*, Baltimore: Johns Hopkins Press.

_____, Richard E. Ayres, and William G. Bowman (1967) "Registration and Voting: Putting First Things First," *American Political Science Review*, (June), pp. 359–79.

Kessel, John H. (1984) *Presidential Campaign Politics*, (Second edition), Homewood, Ill.: Dorsey Press.

Key, V. O., Jr. (1949) *Southern Politics in State and Nation*, New York: Knopf.

_____ (1953) "Partisanship and County Office: The Case of Ohio," *American Political Science Review*, (June), pp. 525–36.

_____ (1955) "A Theory of Critical Elections," *Journal of Politics*, (February), pp. 5–18.

_____ (1956) *American State Politics*, New York: Knopf.

_____ (1958, 1964) *Politics, Parties and Pressure Groups* (4th and 5th Editions), New York: Crowell.

_____ (1959) "Secular Realignment and the Party System," *Journal of Politics*, (May), pp. 198–210.

_____ (1961) *Public Opinion and American Democracy*, New York: Knopf.

Kirkpatrick Evron M. (1971) "Toward a More Responsible Two-Party System: Political Science, Policy Science, or Pseudo-Science," *American Political Science Review*, (December), pp. 965–90.

Kirkpatrick, Jeane (1976) *The New Presidential Elite*, New York: Russell Sage Foundation and Twentieth Century Fund.

_____ (1978) *Dismantling the Parties: Reflections on Party Reform and Party Decomposition*, Washington, D.C.: American Enterprise Institute.

Kousser, J. Morgan (1974) *The Shaping of Southern Politics: Suffrage Restriction and the Establishment of the One-Party South, 1880–1910*, New Haven: Yale University Press.

Ladd, Everett Carll, Jr. (1977a) "The Unmaking of the Republican Party," *Fortune*, (September), pp. 91–102.

_____ (1977b) "The Democrats Have Their Own Two-Party System," *Fortune*, (October), pp. 212–23.

_____ with Charles D. Hadley (1975, 1978) *Transformations of the American Party System* (1st and 2nd Editions), New York: Norton.

Lawson, Kay, editor (1980) *Political Parties and Linkage: A Comparative Perspective*, New Haven: Yale University Press.

Lockard, Duane (1959) *New England State Politics*, Princeton: Princeton University Press.

Long, Norton E. (1962) *The Polity*, Chicago: Rand McNally.

Longley, Charles (1978) "Party Reform and the Republican Party." American Political Science Association Paper.

———— (1980) "Party Reform and Party Nationalization: The Case of the Democrats," Chapter 21 in William Crotty, editor, *The Party Symbol*, San Francisco: Freeman.

Maggiotto, Michael A., and Ronald E. Weber (1978) "Amateurs and Professionals: The Case of the County Party Chairperson." Paper presented at Conference on Political Parties in Modern Societies. Evanston: Northwestern University.

Malbin, Michael J., editor (1980) *Parties, Interest Groups, and Campaign Finance Laws*, Washington, D.C.: American Enterprise Institute.

Mazmanian, Daniel A. (1970) *Class Domination and the Party System in the United States*, St. Louis: Washington University. Unpublished Ph.D. dissertation.

McNitt, Andrew D. (1980) "The Effect of Preprimary Endorsement on Competition for Nominations: An Examination of Different Nominating Systems," *Journal of Politics*, (February), pp. 257–66.

Marvick, Dwaine (1980) "Political Linkage Functions of Rival Party Activists in the United States: Los Angeles, 1969–1974," Chapter 5 in Kay Lawson, *Political Parties and Linkage: A Comparative Perspective*, New Haven: Yale University Press.

Michels, Robert (1962) *Political Parties: A Sociological Study of the Oligarchical Tendencies of Modern Democracy*, New York: Crowell-Collier. (Originally published 1915).

Miller, Warren E., Arthur H. Miller, and Edward J. Schneider (1980) *American National Election Studies Data Sourcebook, 1952–1978*, Cambridge: Harvard University Press.

Morehouse, Sarah McCally (1976) "*The Governor as Political Leader*," Chapter 5, in Herbert Jacob and Kenneth N. Vines, editors, *Politics in the American States*, Boston: Little Brown.

———— (1980) "The Effect of Preprimary Endorsements on State Party Strength." American Political Science Assoication Paper.

———— (1981) *State Politics, Parties and Policy*, New York: Holt, Rinehart and Winston.

Muchmore, Lynn, and Thad L. Beyle (1980) "The Governor as Party Leader," *State Government*, (Summer), pp. 121–24.

National Governors' Association (1981) *Reflections on Being Governor*, Washington, D.C.: NGA Center for Policy Research.

National Municipal League (1965) *Presidential Nominating Procedures in 1964, A State-by-State Report*. Introduction by Paul T. David. New York.

Ogden, Daniel M. Jr. (1961) "Trends in Democratic State Party Organization." American Political Science Association Paper.

Olson, David M. (1971) "Attributes of State Political Parties: An Exploration of Theory and Data," pp. 123–57 in James A. Riedel, editor, *New Perspectives in State and Local Politics*, Waltham: Xerox Publishing Company.

Petrocik, John R., and Dwaine Marvick (1980) "The Influence of Institutional Changes on Delegate Recruitment at National Conventions: Primaries and Insurgents," American Political Science Association Paper.

Phillips, Kevin (1969) *The Emergent Republican Majority*, New York: Arlington.

Piereson, James E. (1977) "Sources of Candidate Success in Gubernatorial Elections, 1910–1970," *Journal of Politics*, (November), pp. 939–58.

Polsby, Nelson W. (1983) *Consequences of Party Reform*, New York: Oxford University Press.

Pomper, Gerald M. (1977) "The Decline of Partisan Politics," pp. 13–38 in Louis Maisel and Joseph Cooper, editors, *The Impact of the Electoral Process*, Beverly Hills: Sage Publications.

Prendergast, William B. (1961) "The Evolution of State Party Organization: The Republicans." American Political Science Association Paper.

Price, David E. (1984) *Bringing the Parties Back*, Washington, D.C.: Congressional Quarterly Press.

Rae, Douglas W. (1967) *The Political Consequences of Electoral Laws*, New Haven: Yale University Press (Revised Edition 1971).

Ranney, Austin (1965, 1971, 1976) "Parties in State Politics," in Herbert Jacob and Kenneth N. Vines, editors, *Politics in the American States*, (1st, 2nd and 3rd Editions), Boston: Little, Brown.

_____ (1975) *Curing the Mischiefs of Faction: Party Reform in America*, Berkeley: University of California Press.

_____ (1983) "The President and His Party." Chapter 5 in Anthony King, editor, *Both Ends of the Avenue: The Presidency, the Executive Branch, and Congress in the 1980s*, Washington, D.C.: American Enterprise Institute.

_____ and Willmore Kendall (1954) "The American Party Systems," *American Political Science Review*, (June), pp. 477–85.

Robeck, Bruce W., James J. Dyer, and Henry J. Woods (1978) *Ballot Access*, (Vol. IV, Brief Summary), Washington, D.C.: Federal Election Commission.

Robinson, Edgar E. (1934) *The Presidential Vote*, Stanford, Calif.: Stanford University Press.

Rosenstone, Steven J., and Raymond E. Wolfinger (1978) "The Effect of Registration Laws on Voter Turnout," *American Political Science Review*, (March), pp. 22–45.

Rusk, Jerrold G. (1970) "The Effect of the Australian Ballot Reform on Split Ticket Voting: 1876–1908," *American Political Science Review*, (December), pp. 1220–238.

_____ (1974) "The American Electoral Universe: Speculation and Evidence," *American Political Science Review*, (September), pp. 1028–049.

_____, and John J. Stucker (1978) "The Effect of the Southern System of Election Laws on Voting Participation. A Reply to V. O. Key, Jr.," Chapter 6 in Joel H. Silbey, Allan G. Bogue, and William H. Flanigan, *The History of American Electoral Behavior*, Princeton: Princeton University Press.

Sabato, Larry (1981) *The Rise of Political Consultants*, New York: Basic Books.

_____ (1983) *Goodbye to Good-time Charlie: The American Governorship Transformed* (2nd Edition), Washington, D.C.: Congressional Quarterly Press.

Scammon, Richard M. (1956) *America Votes*, New York: Macmillan 1956–1958; Pittsburgh: University of Pittsburgh Press, 1959–1964; Washington, D.C.: Congressional Quarterly, 1966 et seqq.

Schattschneider, E. E. (1942) *Party Government*, New York: Rinehart.

_____ (1948) *The Struggle for Party Government*, College Park: University of Maryland.

Schlesinger, Joseph A. (1957) *How They Became Governor*, East Lansing: Michigan State University, Governmental Research Bureau.

_____ (1965) "Political Party Organization." Chapter 18 in James G. March, editor, *Handbook of Organizations*, Chicago: Rand McNally.

_____ (1966) *Ambition and Politics: Political Careers in the United States*, Chicago: Rand McNally.

_____ (1971) "The Politics of the Executive," in Herbert Jacob and Kenneth N. Vines, *Politics in the American States: A Comparative Analysis*, (2nd Edition), Boston: Little, Brown.

Schumpeter, Joseph A. (1942) *Capitalism, Socialism and Democracy*, New York: Harper.

Sorauf, Frank J. (1963) *Party and Representation*, New York: Atherton.

_____ (1975) "Political Parties and Political Analysis." Chapter 2 in William Nisbet Chambers and Walter Dean Burnham, editors, *The American Party Systems: Stages of Political Development*. (2nd Edition), New York: Oxford.

_____ (1980) *Party Politics in America* (4th Edition), Boston: Little, Brown.

Starr, Joseph R. (1940), "The Legal Status of American Political Parties," *American Political Science Review* (June and August), pp. 439–55, 685–99.

Stokes, Donald E. (1975) "Parties and the Nationalization of Electoral Processes." Chapter 7 in William Nisbet Chambers and Walter Dean Burnham, editors, *The American Party Systems: Stages of Political Development*, (2nd Edition), New York: Oxford.

Sundquist, James L. (1973) *Dynamics of the Party System*, Washington, D.C.: Brookings Institution.

Tocqueville, Alexis de (1946) *Democracy in America*, Edited by Phillips Bradley, (2 vols.), New York: Knopf.

Turner, Julius (1951) *Party and Constituency: Pressures on Congress* Baltimore: Johns Hopkins Press. (Revised edition by Edward V. Schneier, Jr., Baltimore: Johns Hopkins Press, 1970.)

Wahlke, John C. (1971) "Policy Demands and System Support: The Role of the Represented," *British Journal of Political Science*, (July), pp. 271–90.

_____ (1979) "Pre-Behavioralism in Political Science," *American Political Science Review*, (March),pp. 9–31.

_____, Heinz Eulau, William Buchanan, and Leroy C. Ferguson (1962) *The Legislative System*, New York: Wiley.

Wattenberg, Martin P. (1981) "The Decline of Political Partisanship in the United States: Negativity or Neutrality?," *American Poliltical Science Review*, (December), pp. 941–50.

Weber, Max (1946) "Bureaucracy" in H. H. Gerth and C. Wright Mills, editors, *From Max Weber: Essays in Sociology*, New York: Oxford University Press.

Weber, Ronald E. (1969) "Competitive and Organizational Dimensions of American State Party Systems." Northeastern Political Science Association Paper.

Wilson, James Q. (1962) *The Amateur Democrat*, Chicago: University of Chicago Press.

Wright, Gerald C., Jr. (1974) *Electoral Choice in America: Image, Party, and Incumbency in State and National Elections*, Chapel Hill: Institute for Research in Social Science, University of North Carolina.

Zeller, Belle (1954), editor, *American State Legislatures*, New York: Crowell.

Index

About the Authors

Cornelius P. Cotter is professor of Political Science at the University of Wisconsin-Milwaukee. He holds an AB from Stanford University and an MPA and PhD from Harvard. He has served in party and governmental staff positions at the national level. His published contributions include books and articles on American party and governmental processes.

James L. Gibson is associate professor of political science at the University of Houston. An University of Iowa Ph.D., Professor Gibson previously taught at the University of Wisconsin-Milwaukee. His research interests are in American politics, with particular emphasis in judicial process and behavior, public opinion and policy, and political parties. His research reports have appeared in the American Political Science Review, the American Journal of Political Science, the Journal of Politics, the Law and Society Review, and elsewhere. He is co-author of a forthcoming book on political tolerance in America.

John F. Bibby is a professor of political science at the University of Wisconsin-Milwaukee and a specialist in party and congressional politics. He also serves as an adjunct scholar of the American Enterprise Institute and is codirector of its Congress Project. He is coauthor of *On Capitol Hill: Studies in the Legislative Process* and *Vital Statistics on Congress*, as well as articles for professional journals and symposia. Bibby has also served in leadership positions of national and state party organizations and in senior staff positions of the House of Representatives.

Robert J. Huckshorn, Dean of the College of Social Science and Professor of Political Science, at Florida Atlantic University, previously taught at UCLA and the University of Idaho, and was Associate Director of the National Center for Education in Politics in New York. He received his Ph.D. in Political Science at the University of Iowa in 1956. He has published six books and numerous articles. He is the President of the Southern Political Science Association representing political scientists in eighteen states. Huckshorn has been a member of the Florida Elections Commission since 1973. In 1984 he was appointed to serve as Interim Dean of the College of Education at FAU and chaired a broadly-based Task Force on Teacher Education.